D1765620

TOWARDS
A
UNITED IRELAND

An Uncompleted Journey

by Billy Leonard

CheckPoint
Press

CONTENTS

To Valerie

COUNTIES OF THE ISLAND OF IRELAND BY PROVINCE 2012

ULSTER
(Northern Ireland): Antrim, Armagh, Derry/Londonderry, Down, Fermanagh, Tyrone.
(Republic of Ireland): Cavan, Donegal, Monaghan.

MUNSTER
(Republic of Ireland): Clare, Cork, Kerry, Limerick, Tipperary, Waterford.

LEINSTER
(Republic of Ireland): Carlow, Dublin, Kildare, Kilkenny, Laois, Lonford, Louth, Meath, Offaly, Westmeath, Wexford, Wicklow.

CONNAUGHT
(Republic of Ireland): Galway, Leitrim, Mayo, Roscommon, Sligo.

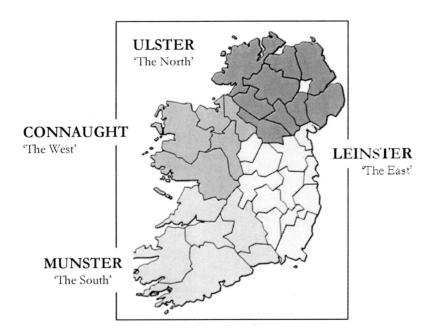

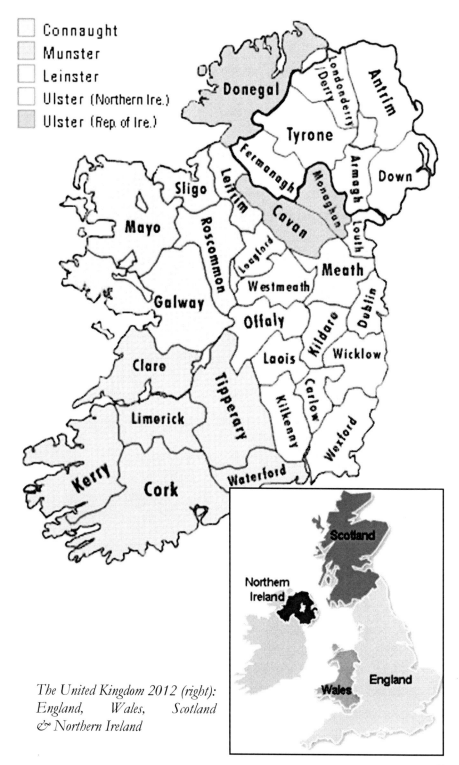

Connaught
Munster
Leinster
Ulster (Northern Ire.)
Ulster (Rep. of Ire.)

Donegal
Londonderry / Derry
Antrim
Tyrone
Fermanagh
Armagh
Down
Sligo
Leitrim
Monaghan
Cavan
Louth
Mayo
Roscommon
Longford
Meath
Westmeath
Galway
Offaly
Dublin
Clare
Laois
Kildare
Wicklow
Tipperary
Carlow
Limerick
Kilkenny
Wexford
Kerry
Cork
Waterford

Scotland
Northern Ireland
Wales
England

The United Kingdom 2012 (right):
England, Wales, Scotland
& Northern Ireland

7

GLOSSARY OF ABBREVIATIONS

BBC – British Broadcasting Corporation

BBC NI – British Broadcasting Corporation, Northern Ireland

BRIC – Brazil Russia India China (collectively referred to as the BRIC countries)

CAL – Culture Arts & Leisure Committee (one of the Departmental Committees in the Northern Ireland Assembly)

Dáil – Irish Parliament

DUP – Democratic Unionist Party

ECB – European Central Bank

EEC – European Economic Community

EU – European Union

FDI – Foreign Direct Investment

FF – Fianna Fáil

FG – Fine Gael

FOI – Freedom of Information

GAA – Gaelic Athletic Association

GB – Great Britain

GFA – Good Friday Agreement

IBEC – Irish Business & Employers Confederation

IFA – Irish Football Association

IMF – International Monetary Fund

INLA – Irish National Liberation Army

IRA – Irish Republican Army (used interchangeably with PIRA – Provisional IRA)

IRB – Irish Republican Brotherhood

MI5 – one of the British intelligence agencies

MLA – Member of Legislative Assembly (Northern Ireland Assembly – often referred to as the Belfast Assembly)

MP – Member of Parliament (British Parliament)

NI/N Ireland – Northern Ireland

NIO – Northern Ireland Office

OFMDFM – Office of the First Minister & Deputy First Minister

OSCE – Organisation for Security & Co-operation in Europe

PM – Prime Minister

PSNI – Police Service of Northern Ireland

PUP – Progressive Unionist Party

RD – Regional Development Committee (one of the Departmental Committees in the Northern Ireland Assembly)

R&D – Research and Development

RTÉ – Radio Teilifís Éireann (Ireland's National Broadcaster)

RUC – Royal Ulster Constabulary

RUCR – Royal Ulster Constabulary Reserve

SAS – Special Air Service

SDLP – Social Democratic & Labour Party

SF – Sinn Féin

SNP – Scottish National Party

STV – Single Transferrable Vote

Taoiseach – Irish Prime Minister

TD – Teachta Dála (member of the Dáil / Irish Parliament)

The North – Northern Ireland

The South – Republic of Ireland

UDA – Ulster Defence Association

UDP – Ulster Democratic Party

UDR – Ulster Defence Regiment

UK – United Kingdom

US – United States of America

USC – Ulster Special Constabulary (part of which was the 'B' Specials)

UTV – Ulster Television

UUP / UU – Ulster Unionist Party

UVF – Ulster Volunteer Force

UWC – Ulster Workers Council

*   *   *

INTRODUCTION

The centenary of the 1912 Third Home Rule Bill in Ireland was marked in April 2012 with the first of many planned events in a decade of commemorations scheduled to run until 2022. The occasion of marking important milestones in Irish history against the international backdrop of 'The Gathering' of the Irish diaspora in Ireland in 2013, is I believe, the perfect opportunity to launch a book that outlines a realistic and pragmatic vision for a united Ireland. We can only hope that the decade of commemorations will provide the Irish people with more hope and inspiration than some of the disquieting socio-political and financial events of recent years.

As I started to write this book in detail, Ireland had just elected a new Fine Gael–Labour coalition government with the political, economic and social parameters firmly set by the International Monetary Fund (IMF), the European Central Bank (ECB) and the European Union in general (EU). The public south of the border are now very well versed in terms such as 'primary bondholders', 'hair-cuts', 'bail-outs', 'burning bond-holders' and 'toxic banks' while some, and I stress *some* north of the border look on with glee, smugly viewing these financial difficulties as verification of their political allegiance to the United Kingdom.

So for me, writing a book advocating a united Ireland in this particular context is quite a challenge. But we must be brave enough to look beyond the immediate context. When one of the great European heroes Václav Havel died there were many fond memories of his prodigious achievements. One described how Havel's participation in the Prague Appeal to western countries to bring down the 'iron curtain' was considered naïve at the time (Jan Kavan in *Irish Times* 19 Dec 2011). But time has proven the doubters wrong and Václav Havel is now seen as one who was capable of seeing through the difficult times, to something better.

I have lived long enough to remember attitudes in the mid-1960s when Unionists articulated their smugness in the rather transitory 'politics of tarmac' whereby the quality of northern roads was sufficient evidence of how better-off they were than their 'poor cousins' in the South. However, the slide into 'the Troubles'; reliance on public service employment while traditional northern industries faded into history; the rise and fall of the 'Celtic Tiger'; and the financial realities of open markets have all changed attitudes many times since. I have therefore no doubt that we will not be tied to recession thinking forever, and we will all move to yet another episode where the parameters will again be different, and will hopefully lead to better times.

On the other hand, some say that we should leave things as they are. Generally, these are people satisfied with a status-quo that employs the multi-party Good Friday Agreement (GFA) as the endgame, a theme to which I will return. However, for reasons that will become clear later in the book, I would be of the alternative school saying this should not be the case. These competing views were strongly reflected during Queen Elizabeth's visit to Ireland in May 2011. Channel Four's Jon Snow interviewed southern writer Sebastian Barry and northern commentator Jude Collins. My impression of the words chosen was that the former contextualised the visit as 'a meeting of Irish and British *equals* in a *settled* political environment', whereas Collins—correctly in my opinion—had to remind viewers that there was still 'the question of the North'.

I therefore believe that as the decade 2012 to 2022 unfolds further, important debates will be held as we commemorate key landmarks in Irish history. The evolving campaign for home rule; the signing of the Ulster Covenant in 1912; the 1916 Easter Rising; the Somme; the 1918 general election; and all the political events of post-First World War Ireland that led to partition and the Irish Civil War will, with many other such events, provide contemporary platforms for reflection and debate. I hope this work will contribute to those discussions.

It is perhaps best to say what this book is not. Readers will I am sure, be relieved to hear that this is not an autobiography. Even with my personal journey from Unionism to Republicanism, I do not flatter myself that there is enough in my life to warrant an entire book. Neither is this an academic work. Despite having worked in that environment—and perhaps because of that experience—I have no desire to restrict myself solely to that type of enterprise, but I do of course hope to bring a certain rigour to the work. Therefore, this book is a personal polemic in the best sense of the term, outlining ultimately my belief that a united Ireland is the best possible solution for our island in the future.

I will of course weave some of my personal experiences into the book as they were shaped in the harsh political realm of a partitioned Ireland. Those experiences came from my direct involvement in northern politics, while at the same time being a follower of politics in the South. Indeed I lived, paid my taxes and voted in a couple of elections in Dublin. I would like to think therefore that my work is well-informed from a generally inclusive 'all-Ireland' basis, and will be received as it is genuinely offered; as a work for the Ireland of the future.

While the main theme of this book is, in my opinion optimistic, positive and forward-thinking, we must nevertheless tackle with frankness and candour some of the more thorny issues that have bedevilled the North of Ireland in particular since the time of partition. I hope that the time I spent living and working in different communities will afford me the licence to offer some sincere critiques, without causing offence or alienation to any particular group, faith or political party. For example, because I was a member of the Royal Ulster Constabulary Reserve (RUCR), then later was involved in Irish Nationalist and Republican politics, I obviously gained a deep knowledge of the Protestant and Catholic communities. I would therefore ask that all readers, from whatever background, evaluate in the spirit of openness, the ideas in this book from an objective perspective that puts the future of Ireland and that of our children first, and places the overall collective good *before* the short-term agendas or political goals of any particular group or creed.

The book begins by outlining some of my personal background so that readers are generally aware of where I am coming from personally, and socio-politically; I will then look back to partition and examine some of the different experiences North and South of the border, as well as reviewing the all-important 'identity question'. Moving on to the often-difficult relationships between political parties who are actually aligned on the ideal of Irish unity, we reveal why certain traditional-historical positions make real cooperation difficult on the bigger-picture issues. Two chapters are then devoted to a vision of what a united Ireland could look like and how we could go about achieving that aim using a strategy of progressiveness, professionalism and pragmatism that draws on the best of the various contributors. I make a central proposal for setting up a non-party-political organisation to drive forward and facilitate much of this work; I will call that body 'Vision Ireland' and further outline a broad strategy for its potential endeavours.

I stress again the importance of working all this through the decade of commemorations and looking beyond the current recession. Ninety years have passed since partition: over the next ten years we can have informed conversations about the future of Ireland, thankfully, now in a peaceful context.

Finally, one does not go through the type of change in Ireland that I have without experiencing various difficulties. I have never dwelt on these and have always placed them in proper perspective, as so many people have had greater difficulties than I have had. However as this book contains a vision that is very important to me, I have to express my deepest gratitude in two particular ways.

Firstly and collectively to my six sons who had the added tension of a political father in a difficult location during their formative years. They always reacted positively to me and more importantly did not negatively react to the difficulties and challenges that were sometimes thrown up to them because of their dad. I say a profound thank-you to Chris, Jamie, Adam, Seán, Marc and Ruaidhrí.

And to my wife who has always been loving, brilliant, supportive and understanding. No-one else will ever know how superb she has been, and that is what makes it such a wonderful privilege to be her husband. I say another profound thank-you to Valerie.

Chapter One

Personal Background

I promised that this book would not be autobiographical, but I think devoting this chapter to outlining my personal and political development and the evolution of my identity will help put a lot of the succeeding pages into a more meaningful context.

I was born into a Protestant and Unionist family. Both my grandfathers were in the Orange Order although each hailed from very different backgrounds, one a South Armagh farmer, the other a Belfast shopkeeper. Interestingly, my farming grandfather's family was just the second Protestant owner of that farm, the first having been the settler-planter family who dispossessed the original Irish owners in the late seventeenth century. The descendants of the dispossessed lived at the edge of the farm right down until the early 1930s. My mother remembered as a small girl the last of that Irish family passing away, and later related the story to me. I was flabbergasted at the very direct link to such an important period of Irish history within my family circle, and tried to imagine the feelings of successive generations of the dispossessed watching 'the planters' farm their land.

I also remember my mother relating to me her father's opinion on the partition of Ireland. Given that his farm was in Armagh and he sold cattle in the neighbouring County Monaghan just down the road, he had lived a life which didn't see any difference between these Ulster counties, yet they ended up in two so-called 'separate' states. He told my mother that he considered Ireland much too small in many ways—including socially and economically—to be partitioned!

My mother became a teacher and met her Royal Ulster Constabulary (RUC) husband when he was posted to a South Armagh police station in the war years. My father was then transferred to Lurgan, where they settled for the rest of their lives. With a little irony I can share that when my Protestant father first arrived in Lurgan to start his work, an RUC 'colleague' refused to meet him at the train and assist with his baggage because with a name like Leonard, he assumed my father would be a Catholic.

It was in that deeply divided Lurgan town that I spent my formative years, where I would be educated, and which I only left after I married my wife Valerie.

My upbringing was therefore a Unionist one, with both parents content with the steady, pensionable state employment. They were part of the generation born immediately after partition and were satisfied with that political situation. I went regularly to the local Presbyterian Church as expected, and attended a 'state' primary school and then the local grammar school. Catholics were as rare as hen's teeth in these establishments except for the last two 'A' level years in grammar school, when a number of Catholic students joined us from other schools. The schools that I attended had that British/Unionist/Protestant ethos marking royal occasions. I remember being lined up to wave our Union Jacks when a young Prince Philip was helicoptered into Lurgan Park, and seeing Protestant Ministers being wheeled into school Assemblies to deliver their sermonettes in rather patronising terms. Meanwhile, our schools had nothing to do with things Irish, such as St Patrick's Day for example.

However, it would be wrong to think that my earlier years were totally isolated from Catholics/Nationalists/Republicans, as I also had friends from that community, particularly in the years immediately prior to the outbreak of 'the Troubles'.

As well as being Unionist/Protestant, I would also describe my upbringing as conservative. My parents were certainly not ultra-conservative, but the small-town, small-community atmosphere and the conservative religious and education systems were all conditioning influences which even at an early age, I strongly resisted. Ironically, it was via international issues that I first noticed how I differed from the local and family authority figures.

I was intrigued by the Martin Luther King era, and remember being incensed at the grainy TV pictures of white policemen beating black civil rights marchers in the US. The images of separate drinking fountains for blacks and whites in some southern US cities astounded me. I also remember a local (and Christian) doctor, who was accepted as the paragon of virtue, education and social standing, being absolutely racist in his attitudes as he discussed with my father the issue of African nations fighting for their independence. I was the 'not to speak until spoken to' young lad listening to these adults but, even at that tender age, I was alert and sensitive enough to be extremely unforgiving in my summation of this so-called 'authority figure' with a stethoscope around his neck. His views were straight from the white-supremacist colonial textbook. It was no surprise that in the following years I would admire the likes of Helen Suzman and Beyers Naudé, both white anti-apartheid activists in South Africa, as people who went against the norm in their community and who stood up for others simply because they believed it was right to do so. It is also therefore no surprise that I was enraged— some years later—when I heard Margaret Thatcher describe Nelson Mandela as "a terrorist" while at the same time upholding Chilean dictator Augusto Pinochet as a good man: it's wonderful the difference a few years make!

My reference to these events very obviously points to my interest in history, politics and current affairs: history was my favourite school subject, and I always felt very comfortable studying it, even more so when it was Irish history. My grammar school history teachers were all what I would regard as Protestant establishment figures, especially my 'A' level teacher. It seemed to me he was playing the soldier-type figure through his commander position in the 'Army Cadet Force'—a more military version of the boy scouts. Somewhat cynically perhaps, I thought it was some sort of substitution for him not having had an army career; that being the authoritarian in a uniform perhaps helped his self-esteem. He taught me the all-important seventeenth century Irish history, and his summary dismissal of the previous Irish social systems pointed to his view that reformation, royalty and plantation were good for Ireland. In short, I was taught Irish history from a British perspective, and I fully appreciate that the other side of that coin is often referred to as the 'Christian Brother' (Irish-Catholic-Nationalist) version of the same history. However, even though I did well in my studies I never totally accepted the school version of Irish history. I remained very interested in the subject, doing my own reading and eventually having a strong Irish history component to my doctoral studies at the University of Ulster.

This natural interest and historical questioning was very important to the evolution of my identity and the development of my political views, especially at a time when the history of the classroom was tragically supplemented by the history of the early 'Troubles' being played out on the streets of Northern Ireland.

As the incidents of unrest increased, and changed from street protests to attacks on the police, I had my first experience of conflict narrowing the field of conversation. Opinions hardened, and even those who usually found it hard to articulate a personal opinion had plenty of them when an attack by Republicans occurred for example, or when a Civil Rights march took place in town. I knew of quite a few friendships between Catholics and Protestants dissolving during these times, as physical division followed mental division.

'The Troubles' witnessed some of the Unionist and Protestant authority figures displaying their true and often dark colours. I remember standing outside the Presbyterian Church when a local (and very well-thought-of) businessman, who was also an Elder in the church, stood with his Bible under his arm addressing the recent disturbances in Lurgan at the time of the Civil Rights marches. His solution was that the police and army should go down the main nationalist streets with their guns and basically shoot where they liked! That attitude obviously spoke volumes to me as a teenager. It was widely understood that one local schoolteacher had a major role in the Ulster Defence Association (UDA). He would later become the local 'warlord' deciding in the 1974 Ulster Workers Council (UWC) strike who could get petrol from the commandeered petrol station in the heart of Unionist/Loyalist Lurgan.

It was also a locally-held belief that a 1975 booby-trap bomb placed in the desk of a primary school office that killed one police officer and seriously injured another was not just part of a burglary as often reported; it was understood to be a direct personal attack on that teacher. I knew the injured policeman, and undoubtedly it seriously affected the rest of his life and that of his wife, who took the burden of all aspects of family life including caring for her husband.

But some of the worst examples of raw sectarian hatred surfaced when the Pope visited Ireland in autumn 1979. Valerie and I were only a few months from our wedding and were out for a quiet Saturday evening drink, on the same day that the Pope addressed a crowd estimated at anything between 200,000 and 300,000 in Drogheda Co. Louth. This is where he made his famous plea for peace. There had been a lot of media coverage of the number of Catholics from the North who travelled the short distance to Drogheda. A Salvation Army Christian came into the lounge selling the denominational paper propagating their Christian worldview. He would have known me and my family name and maybe thought he was on safe ground for voicing his opinion, but he clearly didn't know that Valerie was from a Catholic background. As he offered me a copy of the paper and held his collection box hoping for a donation, he started to lament about how many Catholics had gone to "see the Pope". The whole idea and event was clearly irritating him, but then he added the following in really serious tones: "It's a pity there won't be a few bombs along the road for them returning." Needless to say, he didn't get a donation—we quietly ushered him away—but much more importantly, Valerie was astonished. She wasn't, like many young twenty-plus-year-olds at that time, a practising Catholic, but to hear one alleged Christian representative wanting her co-religionists blown to pieces as they headed home from Mass and the Pope's homily was truly shocking even by Northern standards.

But returning to earlier times, tragic events and attitudes were dreadfully intertwined. A pupil attending my school lost his Ulster Defence Regiment (UDR) father in an IRA gun attack; there was absolute disbelief that this could happen. 'One man one vote' (now one person one vote), was scoffed at in a youth club conversation I heard, and, according to most young Protestants I knew, Civil Rights marchers were mere 'troublemakers'; it followed in their logic that the Ian Paisley's counter-protests were therefore entirely justified, and all the blame for any subsequent trouble was naturally transferred to the Nationalists. When Rev. Ian Paisley walked in front of UDA paramilitaries passing my home, they were in turn headed by a police officer directing traffic to ensure their parade was not hindered; even at that early time in my life I scoffed at how bizarre and perfidious it all appeared. I was also in the classroom when the old Unionist-Stormont regime was prorogued by the British Government in March 1972 just a number of weeks after the shocking events of Bloody Sunday, something, not surprisingly, that wasn't even discussed in my school the day after those murders.

But the first time I was very directly affected, in the sense of family, with the violence of 'the Troubles' was a Saturday morning in the middle of my 'A' level exams in 1972. My father took a phone call and was quickly calling up the stairs that his brother, my uncle Jack, had been shot in his shop on the Crumlin Road in Belfast. An older brother was immediately told to get ready, and he and my father headed off to Belfast. I can remember only a little information coming through during the rest of the weekend. His injuries were serious but not life-threatening, but I remember walking off to my Monday-morning exam without a word from anyone about sitting the exam in this context: it wasn't the generation for counselling, it was quite simply a matter of getting on with it. It later transpired the gunman was a young UDA member who decided to get some money for himself by robbing my grandfather's and uncle's shop. My uncle tried to dash from the shop towards the rear of the building and he was shot in the back. I was told years later that a local UDA leader, who owned a shop nearby, had assured my uncle that his attacker had acted alone without sanction, that he had subsequently been 'dealt with' and wouldn't bother him again. I think my uncle always assumed this meant the robber had been killed by more senior UDA people, and maybe not just solely because of this incident.

The second time violence had quite a direct effect in my family circle was in September 1975. I was making breakfast with my mother, and the early morning news bulletin started to give information about an attack on Orange Lodge members in Tullyvallen, South Armagh. As the basic details (not the names) of the ages and relationship of two of the victims were broadcasted, my mother immediately knew who they were. James and Ronald McKee were her relations and two of five people murdered that night, and my mother was greatly shocked by the killings. Tullyvallen is one of the most remembered incidents of 'the Troubles' and everyone believes the death toll could have been much higher but for an off-duty police officer at the Lodge meeting who returned fire with his personal-issue gun. Republicans carried out the attack, but there is some debate as to whether it was directly the responsibility of the IRA operating under a different name, or, if there was some Irish National Liberation Army (INLA) involvement.

My mother attended the funeral service, and I remember her telling me how sickened she was when Rev. Ian Paisley arrived at the church. She always thought that a lot of the responsibility for 'the Troubles' lay directly at his door.

In company with thousands of others, I too became part of 'the Troubles' generation when we tried to make important local decisions even as the normal societal links between our communities declined, although the links were never completely obliterated as some commentaries have tried to imply. But there is no doubt it was a tremendously bleak time; we tried to convince ourselves we could lead 'normal' lives when in reality, our lives were very far from that.

As the mid-1970s descended into deep conflict, I was starting out in the world of work. There are three events from this period I want to refer to, two of which would have major implications for my life. The first, however, was the virtually inconsequential issue of joining the Orange Order. Although the media loved to point to this period when I later became a Sinn Féin public representative, for me, joining the Orange Order was something of a non-event, although (as I will illustrate later in the book) it did cast up a few very interesting anecdotes. I had joined the Order with a few mates without much thought; over the months and the associated meetings I got totally bored and disillusioned with it, and finally stood up at a meeting to announce my departure.

The second event was much more important. I decided to join the part-time RUC Reserve. As on many other occasions when numbers were needed to supplement the full-time police in troubled times, a part-time force was organised. The RUC Reserve was one leg of the move to replace the infamous 'B' Specials; an almost exclusively Protestant-Unionist 'Special Constabulary' disbanded in 1970. I thought for quite a time about taking this step. A few of my peers had already gone to the paramilitaries. My decision was to go with the law-and-order approach, although it soon became a case of on-the-street learning about the intricacies of the old chestnut question: '*whose* law and order'? I did three tours of duty each week while continuing my full-time work. I will refer later in the book to some of what I regard as important experiences during this time, but overall I can confidently say that this episode was a major learning curve in my relatively young life. I saw the good, the bad and the downright unacceptable of policing in a divided society in those six years as a part-time policeman, and it was definitely important in influencing some of my opinions about the North, and about Ireland as a whole.

The third 'event' was when I started going out with Valerie. As I said earlier, she was from a Catholic background, but the added ingredient was that she lived in the very staunch Republican estate of Kilwilkie in Lurgan. There were therefore certain dangers associated with my part-time police work and Valerie's home location. Undoubtedly I could have been a target, and we also had to think of Valerie's position as an isolated local girl 'going out with one of the enemy'.

I was told by some I was mad, even advised to marry and emigrate to Australia. Clearly, we had to be very careful as to where and when we met. I didn't regularly call at Valerie's home. We met at different times and locations to avoid a routine which would have been a distinct security weakness. On one occasion, I did go to her Kilwilkie home, taking a Tuesday off work, to meet Valerie's mum Kathleen for the first time and have lunch with her. We regarded a mid-week day and time as being a little safer. However, within a few days I got a message from an observant and kindly neighbour via a mutual friend telling me not to take that sort of risk again. We didn't. In fact on the day we got married Valerie didn't even leave for the church from her own family home!

Through my relationship with Valerie, I began to get personal knowledge of how her community saw things in our divided society, which at this stage was in deep conflict. Her father Jim had converted to Catholicism when he married Valerie's mother Kathleen; he was ostracised by his birth family at that point and would relate to his children that he never appreciated what discrimination was until he became a Roman Catholic. It was only then that he saw the real scale of unemployment in Nationalist/Republican areas and the consequent lack of money in families around him. He never had a problem with the police before his marriage and conversion, but he did afterwards. One key event was during the Ulster Workers Council strike in 1974, when the North was in chaos with illegal Loyalist road-blocks; businesses closed by intimidation; people threatened because they defied the strike by trying to get to work; and petrol stations commandeered by Loyalist paramilitaries. It was on one such occasion that a policeman 'booked' Valerie's father for double parking in one of Lurgan's broadest streets as he collected gas! Jim died very suddenly at the early age of 47 within a few weeks of that encounter, and the summons to appear in court for his 'crime' was brought to the house by police officers after his death. He actually died from a heart attack in his local Gaelic Athletic Association (GAA) club in which he played a large role. I never met the man but heard a lot about him from Valerie, who followed in her dad's footsteps helping out at the busy GAA youth club. Overall, while it was a dangerous time, it was also an intriguing time for me as I was a questioning and observant member of the Unionist establishment while gaining a lot of knowledge of a community largely antagonistic to that establishment.

At one point in the late 1970s I noticed a report in a local paper about a certain John Robb of the New Ireland Movement. The fact that he was from a Protestant background and was prepared to put his head above the parapet on the Movement's view on Irish unity impressed me. By that stage I was strongly of the opinion that we had to look beyond Northern Ireland to the entire island to get the solution, and Robb was courageously articulating a version of that view. However, I have to admit I didn't follow up the interest at the time, but curiously I met John some twenty years later and we have enjoyed numerous conversations on Irish history and politics since.

All these personal and state-policing experiences (some of which I refer to later in the book) combined with my historical interest, meant that as we entered the 1980s I was moving inexorably towards what I have often described as being 'a very contented Irishman'. The schizophrenic experience of being 'Irish on holiday, but British at home', or labelling oneself as 'being British' as a specific 'anti-Irish' statement, waned completely for me. And as I have also previously said, my full acceptance of an Irish identity was never a negative or antagonistic commentary on things British or, towards those people who regard themselves as British. It was simply a case of me responding sincerely and thoughtfully to my own experiences in context of a very challenging socio-political environment.

Another event encapsulates this identity evolution. When Republican hunger striker Bobby Sands was elected Member of Parliament (MP) for Fermanagh South Tyrone in 1981, I was attending a family member's funeral. The election count result came through as many of us milled around the deceased's home after the funeral. I remember many furious reactions to this very significant outcome. One of the strongest statements came from a Unionist who was totally convinced that there were over 30,000 voters in Fermanagh South Tyrone who supported terrorism. I, on the other hand, now understood the situation very differently: to life-time Nationalists and Republicans that vote was very understandable. But for those coming from a Unionist background and therefore *not* being part of the tap root of Republican struggle, protest and hunger striking, it was obviously a different picture. In addition I knew then that I was seeing things very differently from possibly all within that particular Unionist/Protestant group that afternoon.

I make these points about my identity now because all else flows from there. My later political involvement was premised on my identity as an Irishman wanting to make a contribution; my political disenchantment with the Social Democratic & Labour Party (SDLP) and decision to join Sinn Féin (SF), as the only main political party organised on an all-Ireland basis, was totally based on my aspirations for Ireland, something I will expand on later. However, I will now refer to how both parties viewed me as one from a Unionist/Protestant background.

There were a lot of members from both parties who gave me great support and got on with the politics rather than worrying about the religion. However, some in the SDLP made too much of the religious label and, as I had already jettisoned all such pigeon-holes, I found that tiresome. The worst was when I was preparing to enter my first electoral contest in 2001. A senior long-time member of the party in East Derry told me that I shouldn't enter because I was 'the wrong sort' apparently, a reference to my religious background. At the other end of the scale, when I attended my first SDLP party conference, Alasdair McDonnell— who became party leader in November 2011—introduced me to many of the party hierarchy as well as visiting politicians from England and southern Irish parties as 'one from the other side' which in contrast, appeared to be a trophy-like approach. The religious label also surfaced in other unconstructive ways, such as when I was accused by another member of 'playing the religious card'. This occurred when I was competing with that person for an internal position. This shows how easy such attitudes can surface when internal competition comes to a head. Interestingly, it was in the same context within Sinn Féin that the worst sectarian attitudes against me were displayed. I was in a tough competition to win an internal vote for a position in the party when a trusted colleague told me in very frank terms how two members in particular were scathing in their sectarian description of me. I believe there were others involved as well. So, from within both parties I saw how easy attitudes can harden in the age-old sectarian way, especially when you put yourself forward competing for positions and trying to get support from others. And at a grass roots level there were many 'shinners' who reverted to the 'orange B' description of Unionists/Protestants at the drop of the hat.

However, I have to say that the only time I experienced the sectarian head-count principle being applied was when I canvassed in East Derry elections with a senior member of the SDLP. When I suggested canvassing certain homes where the people were more likely to be Unionist and/or Protestant, she quickly described it as a waste of time, that we had to approach it as a sectarian head-count and get the 'Catholic vote' out.

But there was an additional dimension within Sinn Féin. Trusting an ex-RUC Reservist was far more than just a question of me coming from a Protestant background, and there were differing attitudes. Some were very welcoming and reminded me that I wasn't the first from the security forces that had moved to Republicanism. Some were very trusted colleagues who supported me in very practical ways, but there were of course some who saw it differently. When I gave a talk in Belfast as part of a festival week, I was told by Laurence McKeown (one of the 1980s Maze hunger strikers) that one Republican steadfastly refused to come to the event, saying that he wouldn't have anything to do with me. I was also told that I was lucky being based in East Derry, that had I been in one of several other constituencies there was 'no way' that I would have been accepted. In addition, a long-time RTÉ journalist informed me he knew from his many contacts in the party that there was a lot of suspicion about me joining SF and numerous members were hostile to me.

I record these issues which relate to both parties now, to simply show that while I may have many challenging things to say about Unionism, I also have to be fair across the board and say that there are still journeys to be travelled by many within Nationalism/Republicanism in order to really put sectarianism to bed. True Republicanism cannot be sectarian in any shape or form, and Nationalism cannot be the nationalism of any one faith or creed. But let us maintain hope and confidence in the knowledge that even since these events occurred improvements are happening. There is an imperative for all of us to rise above the 'isms', be they sectarian, racist or any other type.

But there were broader and equally challenging issues which relate to my time in Sinn Féin from 2004–11.

Undoubtedly I met people in Sinn Féin who were major players in 'the Troubles', many who lost relatives and friends during those years and were genuinely committed to the political path. I knew such people at both constituency and central level and there were many examples of good attitudes and actions never conveyed by the media or, which rightly happened away from the glare of publicity. However, there were also examples of that difficult tension between the long-established 'army' approach, and the political path.

When I became a member of the party, I had to ride out the immediate publicity about, and the reactions to my decision. However, the first really bigger-picture issues were the December 2004 Northern Bank robbery in Belfast which netted £26 million, and the January 2005 murder of Robert McCartney after a fight in a Belfast bar. Internal SF reaction to the bank raid was interesting to say the least. There was deep ambivalence and cynical laughter among many, but also deep anger by some party members who obviously saw the bigger picture. One of those furiously declared to me that there were people in 'the movement' who simply weren't aware of, and maybe didn't even give a damn, about the long and difficult work involved in politics. No one believed the largest bank raid in Irish and British history was carried out by anybody other than Republicans, but the most bizarre reactions came at a meeting held in Derry to inform SF members of the 'political line' to be taken and how the party would ride out the media storm. One member said from the floor that he didn't want to believe it was anyone other than Republicans as that would mean there was another group with similar 'professional expertise': there was laughter across the hall.

But the mirth of the night betrayed deeper issues as did the McCartney murder, which had led—directly or indirectly—to the suspension of a number of SF members. There were obviously people affiliated with Sinn Féin/Republicanism who weren't capable of seeing the larger political picture, who felt they were above the hard graft of political representatives and of those who supported their day-to-day work. A calculated bank robbery and a drunken brawl after some had attended the Bloody Sunday anniversary march are hardly the work of those with political vision. And if the bank robbery was a group running solo then where was the internal discipline? Or, if not 'solo' then what was the relationship between the robbers and others? In addition there was the Belfast syndrome. Many SF party members were privately very critical saying there were too many Belfast people who thought they could do as they pleased and would not be dealt with by the mainly 'Belfast' leadership.

During the long-running reaction to both these incidents, I was announced as Sinn Féin's Westminster candidate and also a candidate for the local elections to Coleraine Borough Council, both in May 2005. I met with a senior Sinn Féin official to discuss the Westminster candidacy and, when I said that our mission to keep increasing our percentage vote in East Derry was not helped by people robbing banks and murdering people, he was quite taken aback. His reaction was tame, simply saying the party had been through worse situations and we would just have to accept the context, and do our best. He offered no criticism whatsoever of both incidents. I know for definite these incidents seriously harmed our campaign. I met enough people who were honest enough to say that they had no problem with me personally as the candidate, but both the seriousness of the issues and the ambivalence and lack of any real action by Sinn Féin, meant they could not vote for me.

The tensions between the long tentacles of 'army' approaches, the ingrained loyalties that extended from 'the Troubles' and the evolution to politics, manifested themselves in many ways. When the IRA finally ordered an end to its armed campaign in July 2005, I had a conversation with Dominic Adams, brother of SF President Gerry Adams. He genuinely expressed to me that the 'historic' decision to disarm left him feeling strange, as he felt the defence for his community had now gone. I found Dominic to be a quiet-spoken, reflective person, so I always regarded that opinion as sincere, and certainly not just some Republican jingoism. Within a few months the decommissioning of 'all' weapons as witnessed by two clergymen, was met with anger by many SF party members who thought that the IRA should never give in to the demands of Unionists and the British on weapons. Many of those who were most angry were non-combatants, whether through non-involvement or simply being too young to have been involved. When the IRA was finally disbanded in September 2008, the one remaining link that kept many in the party only relatively happy was the fact that the Army Council stayed in place.

As one who came from the outside, I always found interesting the whole spectre of central leadership, Army Council and the 'democratic structures' of Sinn Féin. One elected Member of the Legislative Assembly (MLA) in Belfast expressed to me in very open terms that he knew who really held the power in the party, and accepted that this was the best way to get on with the work. In essence he knew that the elected representatives didn't hold the real power, rather it was held by a blend of Ardchomhairle and Army Council members: everyone was meant to be equal but in classical terms some were more equal than others. In that context I found the unending references to 'the leadership' and 'referring issues to the leadership' somewhat amusing. On the one hand we were told the local cumann (branch) and comhairle cheantair (constituency organisation) could make their own decisions, but at the end of the day all the little networks with ex-army personnel on those local structures meant that divergence from the leadership either didn't happen or, could be quickly corrected. Internal democracy was often massaged to put the 'right people' in the important positions, and during my time the 'right people' were still mostly ex-army.

This ambivalence between army and political elements was particularly clear when it came to an issue in my constituency of East Derry as I started my work as an MLA in January 2010. One of the leading members Sean McGlinchey had been 'stood down' just before Christmas 2009. Who actually stood him down became a moot question. There was uproar as Sean was a very popular member. He served time for bombing Coleraine, came from a strong Republican family which included Dominic McGlinchey and worked very hard, particularly in the Dungiven area. East Derry Sinn Féin members then had to sit in a Sinn Féin office being addressed by two senior Sinn Féin members who said the standing-down was not a Sinn Féin action! But neither of the two 'leadership' figures would say who stood him down and what for: it was totally bizarre and the elephant in the room was never named!

This type of incident, including higher-profile episodes such as the fall-out from Denis Donaldson's outing as a British agent, and his subsequent April 2006 murder, as well as the seemingly-endless 'unofficial' meetings between key constituency personnel (mostly ex-army) and 'the leadership' of Sinn Féin, led to some distrust and frankly, often to the question, who do you believe? When one considers that some of those in relatively important local party positions had, in the opinion of many, little political prowess, it is easy to conclude that various tensions affected the day-to-day politics within the party particularly when it came to election planning and strategies. I stress these were important points in East Derry: I don't know the detail from other constituencies, but similar feelings from other areas were, from time-to-time expressed to me.

But at the same time, when the leadership wanted to move a significant issue forward, they could very effectively get discussion moving at what were called in my area 'family meetings'. These were much broader than cumann/branch meetings and included activists of all kinds down through the years. Senior party figures could be produced to address these meetings and this method was used extensively in the policing debate which ended with the January 2007 decision by Sinn Féin to accept, and enter the policing structures in the North. These were the only meetings in which I heard real dissent by those who held strong opinions on this crucial issue, and admittedly, party figures handled everything well. When it came to the actual Ard Fheis debate and vote it was noteworthy that very senior Republican families—some of whom had lost relatives during the conflict—were selected to speak in favour of the motion.

So out of these bigger-picture experiences that I personally witnessed, and the many other issues in early twenty-first century Irish politics, it is clear that Sinn Féin is now on the move, evolving from what it regards as a war, but still with some features of the centralism and loyalties of the established 'army' approach. I personally think this has to evolve further and I will take up some more specific issues about Sinn Féin and the other parties in the context of working for a united Ireland later in the book.

But for now the focus in the next chapter will be on partition.

Chapter Two

Partition

From the 1870s to 1920, the debate about 'Home Rule' was the single most dominant feature of Anglo-Irish political life. Essentially, Home Rule was the method by which it was hoped that Ireland could be reconciled to the British Empire. An 'Assembly' in Ireland consisting of two chambers would conduct Ireland's internal affairs, while the United Kingdom Parliament at Westminster retained control of areas such as foreign policy, armed forces, security and major taxation policies. With some exceptions the Liberals in England, initially under William Gladstone, supported Home Rule while their rivals the Conservatives, opposed it. In Ireland, Irish Nationalists worked strenuously for the ideal while Unionists opposed it fearing their position as a minority—and mainly Protestant group—would leave them open to control by a strongly Roman Catholic led country. The vagueness of the term 'Home Rule' as it was debated through the decades also created difficulties. As Republicanism in Ireland gained political strength with an evolving campaign for a free Irish republic it became clear that 'Home Rule' would not deliver enough for them.

Different players with vastly different political goals meant the overall fifty-year journey to 'Home Rule' and partition was arduous, with many twists and turns. The considerable extension of the franchise for the all-important 1885 and 1886 Westminster elections and the first Home Rule Acts of 1886 and 1893 were the building blocks to a period that witnessed astonishing changes in Ireland. There were also major changes across Europe and other parts of the world where lines were drawn on maps by masters of empires. These were meant to be solutions but unfortunately, and many times predictably, only led to further difficulties.

Those who would interpret history retrospectively in an effort to validate their political allegiances and conditioning might argue that the division of Ireland into two separate entities comprising 6 and 26 counties was inevitable. But this is not the case. Reading history backwards is unfortunately a regular habit in the North. It is bad enough for so-called senior politicians in the Belfast Assembly to fall into this trap when speaking, for example, about 'Northern Ireland in 1916' when it obviously didn't exist, but it is worse again when educators regularly make similar statements, as I have personally witnessed. The bigger tragedy is they didn't even appreciate the point.

I am not going to give a comprehensive account of the decades of history leading to partition. It is readily available in numerous excellent publications which have been crafted to do that very thing. I have though relied mainly on two works which refreshed my memory about the many historical twists and turns, but also give some good commentary on the political compromises and contradictions of the period. They are JJ Lee's acclaimed book *Ireland 1912-1985: Politics and Society* (Cambridge University Press, 1989) and Diarmaid Ferriter's excellent work *The Transformation of Ireland 1900-2000* (Profile Books, 2004).

The first key point to note is that Irish Unionism didn't want Home Rule of *any* kind never mind a partitioned Ireland. Theirs was a campaign in context of being part of the British Empire, desiring to remain within that empire ruled from its centre, England. The well-known quote 'Home Rule is Rome rule' epitomises the sectarian fear behind the Unionist tactic; they dreaded Home Rule from Dublin where indigenous people voted for their own Parliament, and in which Unionists would be a minority voice instead of being aligned with the mighty British Empire. Ferriter is ultimately correct when he says that the Unionists may not have wanted Home Rule, but unfortunately the Empire did.

The Home Rule stakes were particularly raised when the Parliament Act of 1911 removed many of the legislation-blocking powers of the House of Lords and thereby asserted the supremacy of the House of Commons in London. This meant that the Tory-dominated House of Lords in London would no longer be able to move against Home Rule. The issue now had to be resolved by the elected British parliament much to the chagrin of Irish Unionists. But the Unionists had 'friends' whose London/English/Empire agenda would be helped by continuing the fight against this constitutional reform, most notably the Conservative party. One key player was the Tory leader Andrew Bonar Law who used the Home Rule issue to maximum effect. He played the Empire card, saying the Empire would be in peril if Ireland got its way, and thus increased the political pressure on the Liberal supporters of Home Rule in the British Parliament. He sought an election on the Home Rule issue and wasn't afraid to stir the Unionist masses at a major rally in Balmoral, Belfast in 1912. The subsequent signing of the Ulster Covenant, as well as the Ulster Unionist Council decision to deny the right of any people, including a British Government, to impose Home Rule were also significant milestones. Irish Unionism's 'democratic credentials' were severely compromised at this time. They were further diminished as this was the era of Ulster Volunteer Force (UVF) growth (established January 1913) which witnessed many 'law and order' unionists again, compromising this laudable concept.

These events were all pivotal to the tactic of trying to block Home Rule *per se* not just Home Rule for Ulster. It has to be stressed that the wording of the Ulster Covenant spoke of using all means necessary to "defeat the present conspiracy to set up a Home Rule parliament in Ireland". The fact that some of the more fervent signatories to the Ulster Covenant signed in their own blood, illustrates the strength and depth of the passions involved.

Even the context of the First World War (1914-18) and the Dublin Easter Rising (1916) did not materially change the core questions of constitutional reform, Home Rule for Ireland and how Unionism would fight against it. Please note I say the "core questions": the reaction of Unionists, particularly those who fought in World War I may have further hardened, but the war did not mean the questions were put to bed. They weren't: Britain's game plan may have been disastrous, but they did not renege on pursuing how they could progress the central question of Home Rule in the aftermath of war. The sacrifice of many Unionists at the Somme and elsewhere is often seen by succeeding generations of Unionists as proof of their willingness to fight for Britain and the Empire, and therefore how 'different' (and therefore more loyal) they were, thus validating partition. But thankfully it is now recognised that countless Irish men and women also sacrificed their lives in the First World War, many of whom most probably supported Home Rule for all of Ireland and believed, or hoped, that it would be delivered.

As the myriad issues at play unfolded, one of the crucial issues which I believe sums up many of the weaknesses of partition is, ironically, the province of Ulster itself. The idea of a 'covenant' is cherished by Unionists and is of course graphically characterised by the 1912 signing of the Ulster Covenant. The original Unionist tactic at the Buckingham Palace Conference of 1914 was for the inclusion of all nine counties of the province in any act of partition; in fact Edward Carson of the Irish Unionist Alliance accepted that a nine-county Ulster would either be included or excluded in its entirety. However, as things worked out, it was clear that the Unionist covenant with the Protestants of Counties Donegal, Cavan and Monaghan was not so strong as in the remaining six Ulster counties; the subsequent compromises and betrayals by Irish Unionism of their fellow Unionists in these three counties epitomise some of the profound ambivalences that underpinned partition.

Joe Lee presents a very concise number of points which I have gleaned from his book and with which I find it hard to disagree. I also believe it would be difficult for many Unionists to reject them.

Lee claims the Government of Ireland Act 1920 that created Northern Ireland represented capitulation by the British cabinet to Ulster Unionist pressure. The contract between Unionist leader Edward Carson and the Unionist/Protestant minded men and women of Donegal, Monaghan and Cavan was truly broken when those counties were excluded; Catholic majorities in Fermanagh & Tyrone were greater than Protestant majorities in Derry and Armagh; Unionists conceded the North Monaghan constituency which had 33% Protestants but insisted on the South Armagh constituency which had 32% Protestants; Unionists also conceded the East Donegal constituency with 40% Protestants.

Lee continues by saying that Unionist claims to the effect that this was the only democratic solution seem difficult to reconcile; in fact, the decision to concede the three counties provided Unionists with as much territory as they could safely control, and delivered Protestant-Unionist supremacy over Catholic-Nationalists even in predominantly Catholic areas. Lee also rebuts the erroneous argument that the border was devised 'because two peoples could not live together in peace'; the author correctly claims partition brought two warring groups *together* in the North, more than it separated them.

All these points are valid and powerful in highlighting some of the central inconsistencies which gave rise to partition and the creation of Northern Ireland, and the final point is particularly strong but simultaneously tragic. We do not need to work with the hindsight of 'the Troubles' to realise just how politically unworkable the Unionist administration in the North was, and the results it set in train and presided over. I have spoken to many people who lived in the first few post-partition decades; they testified to the societal tensions, the infamous 'Unionist siege mentality' allied to supremacy attitudes which caused many Nationalist/Republican grievances. There are many examples of such attitudes, but one that stuck with me was a very local case and certainly not the usual type recorded in other books. A Lurgan shop had a notice in the window saying Catholics need not apply for jobs, yet the same shop stocked school uniforms for the main Catholic school in the town. Catholics were good enough to give the owner trade and profit, but were not good enough to work there! Being Irish in the North was a second-class existence.

I have purposely used the phrase 'being Irish in the North' at this stage of the book because I firmly believe the simplicity of labels has led to superficial and misleading analysis that has suited some, but served no-one. For example, for many years we have had the constant drip of commentary that the North has a sectarian problem and if only the 'two tribes' could live peacefully, be more tolerant and inclusive, all would be fine. That enables people, north and south of the border and in Great Britain, to see things as an internal problem: this is not—and has never been—just an internal problem. Of course sectarianism has been a disgusting reality, many times played out with tragic results, but it has been used as a convenient byword to avoid dealing with a much more profound problem.

For example, people who belonged to that most Irish of all institutions, the GAA, were many times treated like second-class citizens. I personally know of many supporters and teams travelling to matches that were stopped by the RUC and deliberately delayed for no apparent reason.

35

Some northern media outlets wouldn't even report on their games. The now defunct *Ireland's Saturday Night* sports paper continued right to its final edition refusing to cover anything of GAA games. The GAA organisation was also excluded from public funding opportunities, and I will later refer to my own experience on Coleraine Borough Council in this context. However, when one considers that despite First Minister and DUP leader Peter Robinson attending a GAA match, we had the former Ulster Unionist party leader Tom Elliot still refusing in 2010 to attend such a game, one can see that the North is not just about religious labels. It is, as Brian Feeney put it, an "ethno-political problem" (*Irish News* 13 April 2011): it is, among many things, primarily about the challenges of being Irish in the North.

We all know that gerrymandering constituencies, housing allocation and 'one man one vote' were central issues when 'the Troubles' were brewing, but the malaise went even deeper than those particular difficulties. The genesis of all this was partition. People were clearly not kept apart, but were in fact corralled into what many saw as a false entity—in the sense of normal democracy and shared ambition—with a large schism in a small population. It not only rendered a Unionist majority but also, a sizeable Nationalist/Republican minority community which was in fact too sizeable for permanent and safe domination. Unionist reliance on a 1920 number-crunch could not hold back the rise of an educated population and of more liberal principles of equality. The festering sores grew over a period of time and the inevitable socio-political fractures happened. While it would be difficult to say that the extent of 'the Troubles' was totally predictable, the society that partition 'made' had not—and still doesn't have—enough shared ambition to be truly successful.

The ironic tragedy is that at the time of partition, Unionists did not actually like the 'solution' of partition imposed upon them by the British Government, and were not at all shy at the time articulating that they felt they were caught up in bigger-picture English-and-Empire-politics.

Many people will have heard of Edward Carson's reaction in his speech in the House of Lords in December 1921. The leader of Irish Unionism exclaimed,"what a fool was I" and described himself, Ulster and Ireland itself as "puppets" in the game of getting the Tories into government. A lesser-known reaction, but nonetheless a very illuminating one, is recorded by Diarmaid Ferriter: Lady Lilian Spender, wife of Wilfred Spender who had commanded the UVF, was perfectly positioned in the Unionist campaign to see events unfolding. Lady Spender said she "never really believed England would do this thing" [partition]. She regarded it as reward for Irish treachery, treason and crime of all kinds; she also thought England had penalised their loyalty in passing the Act and didn't want the Unionists. These are hardly views which point to successive Unionist generations seeing partition as somehow inevitable, understandable or natural, and regarding the North as being totally different from the rest of Ireland or even God-ordained, as some have claimed.

To emphasise the point in a historical context: partition was *not* the result that Irish Unionism—which became Ulster Unionism—wanted.

The Partitioning of Experiences

The newly-partitioned parts of Ireland did not go their distinct paths overnight. Trenchant disagreements over what London was actually giving, the failed Boundary Commission and the eventual collapse of The Council of Ireland all meant a period of transition marked by uncertainty, fear and death, most tragically in the Irish Civil War and the Belfast pogroms. Financial arrangements, Ireland's status in relation to London and retention of port access for the British, as well as many other factors, rendered years of difficulty and challenge.

Again my purpose is not to chronicle the detail; that is not the thrust of this book. I have adopted a different approach to highlight how partition resulted in different experiences, South to North and *vice versa*. My examination will run into the next two chapters.

The South was always going to face many 'Everest-sized' challenges. The well-established spirit of independence that had sprouted under British rule now had to face the harsh reality of being a small agrarian economy on the periphery of Europe. One of the greatest achievements in the South was actually surviving the deep-rooted impact of the Irish Civil War. Over a period of time the South established key political structures and public service organisations. The Dáil (the new Parliament in the South) was able to survive a key power transition to de Valera's Fianna Fáil (FF) from Cosgrave's Cumann na nGaedhael in 1932. The import of this should never be underestimated. One civil-war enemy democrat-ically handed power over to another civil-war enemy without military influence, in an era that provided examples such as Poland and Yugoslavia, which did not achieve this democratic fundamental. A state army, a civilian police service, An Garda Síochána, all became firmly established in the South and a civil service took its proper place in society. There were of course still many steps before the South became a republic and left the British Commonwealth, but the organs of state did become firmly embedded.

There were many difficulties in the South during this period, including how Protestants felt in this Roman Catholic-dominated country, and debates still occur on whether killings of Protestants in Cork and other counties were sectarian. These debates have been given fresh impetus by, for example, the very powerful RTE programme An Tost Fada (The Long Silence, 16 April 2012). It gave the account by Canon George Salter of how his Protestant family was forcibly moved out of Cork in April 1922 and also how his father received a deathbed confession of sectarian murder by a local IRA man. Undoubtedly, over the years the Protestant population in the South declined. However, as Protestants, particularly in Dublin, have said to me, they held a privileged and disproportionate role in business and the professions in the South for numerous years. As time went on, many were very relaxed about becoming strong Irish citizens in this new state. I also think Protestants in the North sometimes exaggerate the negatives of the status-quo for their co-religionists in the South, relying on past experiences rather than on contemporary facts. This was highlighted by Protestant Labour TD for Dublin Mid-West Robert Dowds, who confronted northern Protestant sceptics by saying southern Protestants had 'moved on' and in addition, those who voted for him in the South were basically disinter-ested in his religious label (*Irish Times*, 21 March 2012).

The North was of course a different story. Even with its industries it was never able to make a net contribution to the British Exchequer; rather it has always been subsidised. In December 1922 Unionists moved quickly to opt out of the Treaty clause allowing them to join with the South. Despite Unionist disappointment at what they saw as Home Rule of sorts, their leader James Craig lost no time getting plans drawn up for a new home for his 'Protestant parliament for a Protestant people'. This was of course Stormont, an establishment I worked in as an Assembly member. This imposing building was more suited to 1930s Germany rather than the 1930s administration headquarters for a small region that includes 'the dreary steeples of Fermanagh and Tyrone'. Every corner and brick of that building epitomises an attitude of unwarranted Unionist superiority, which actually delivered division based on majoritarianism premised on an artificial majority. Ironically, by the time I served in it, Peter Robinson of the Democratic Unionist Party (DUP) was First Minister in the power-sharing Assembly, and Sinn Féin's Martin McGuinness was Deputy First Minister. Robinson's Unionist political predecessors were responsible for misrule, bad governance and grave mistakes in handling the mainly Nationalist/Republican fight-back via the early Civil Rights Movement of the 1960s. On the other hand, McGuinness's milder political predecessors had had no real effect in Stormont, but there were always more radical Nationalist elements willing to fight to bring about Stormont's downfall, a political strategy that would later be adopted by Martin McGuinness himself.

In addition to 'central government' in the North, the police and civil service did not come from and therefore failed to be integrated into, all sections of the community. Policing became one of the most contentious matters. A predominantly Protestant/Unionist RUC backed up by the infamous 'B' Specials, which were only disbanded in 1970, were in the main, organs of the state definitely perceived and acting as pro-Unionist and anti-Nationalist/Republican. Some individual officers or their families may be angered by that description because of their individual outlook, but I feel history has already judged the accuracy of this narrative and is seen by many as totally self-evident. It wasn't until after the 1999 Patten recommendations were mostly implemented and the Police Service of Northern Ireland (PSNI) was established, that the potential for policing change was in place. At the time of writing much has been achieved, but much more needs to be done. Likewise, local government officials and the Civil Service were predominantly Protestant/Unionist, especially in senior positions. People in my generation spoke of the 'green ceiling'. This essentially evoked the invisible 'glass ceiling' that prevented women from getting higher positions in organisations because of their gender: it was the same for many Nationalists and Republicans in the North.

So, whereas the bigger-picture issues in the South calmed and settled over those important first decades after partition, the North became a 'factory of grievances' as succinctly captured by Patrick Buckland in his book; (*The factory of grievances: devolved government in Northern Ireland, 1921-39*, Gill and Macmillan, 1979). However, I believe the effect of partition goes deeper and is more protean than this brief bigger-picture approach has outlined. I will therefore refer to aspects of nation or state building in the South before devoting the next chapters to the North.

Nation or State Building

My reference to nation or state here has political overtones which I want to deal with briefly. Of course there are many Irish people who say that the Irish nation is not complete while Ireland is partitioned. They will view the nation as being more than the 26 counties of the Republic in terms of those people who reside in the North and view themselves as Irish. Others will, justifiably in my opinion, stretch the concept of the nation further to include the diaspora Irish dotted around the world. This is a 'community' that we are now better aware of thanks largely to the efforts of previous Irish President Mary Robinson. However, we still haven't given either the Northern or the diaspora Irish a vote for the office of President as a concrete demonstration of their respective inclusion in that nation. Other Irish in the South are quite at ease with thinking in terms of the Republic as a completed entity and are satisfied with looking upon it as their state which stops at the border. I recall many irksome occasions for Nationalists/Republicans in the North, when hearing Fine Gael representatives from the South, and Progressive Democrats (when they existed) always talking about 'the State' as if intimating exclusion of all those living North of the border.

Despite the occasional attraction of this debate, I will use the terms 'nation' and 'state' interchangeably, as the purpose of this book is not to decide the 'correct' approach definitively but to propose a broader position.

I would propose that, despite all the recent difficulties in the Irish Republic, especially the dreadful 2007 recession, banking scandal and the outing of rogue senior politicians by the March 2012 Mahon Tribunal (and others), the people of the South have had the privilege of charting their own course and building their own state. Taking responsibility for one's own affairs through the decades was much the better proposition than being under rule from England. Their privilege is a far greater one than the position in the North. Unionist political dominance was clearly wrong, and even in post-Good Friday Agreement Northern Ireland, there is only a perfunctory accommodation of power-sharing, leaving an ethno-political divide still causing difficulties. I will expand on this in the next chapter.

I know that readers from the South will have many criticisms of the Irish State in the time after partition. There were the early financial struggles, and poor standards of housing and health provision; the longer wait for modernisation of services and economic approaches; the overriding social control of the Catholic Church buoyed by the piety of thousands of its members only to be let down by extraordinary and depressing clerical sex abuse scandals; abuses of political power including the brown-envelope culture and excessive salaries whereby the Irish Taoiseach was paid more than the US President; the more recent bursting of the 'Celtic Tiger' bubble in the recession and banking crisis; the questions of sovereignty not only in the straightforward context of membership of the EU but also in the punitive context of the 2010 ECB and IMF loan 'deals': the list could be expanded.

However, giving itself the power to make decisions through its own people and political offices; being internationally recognised in its own right; and negotiating and taking positions in its own right, are all complete statements of independence not to be dismissed or belittled, even in difficult times. Even if there have been abuses of power, mistakes or exceptional learning curves, the right to correct and make good the negative and build on the positives, for the people by the people, is a political position to be cherished, protected and continually renewed. Let me try to illustrate with a blend of some personal thoughts from experiences and practical examples.

My family was certainly not one of those northern Protestant stereotypes that never crossed the border. In fact in terms of day trips and holidays we saw quite a bit of Donegal, the east coast counties and Dublin. But despite this, and regretfully, I still think of myself as one who was cut off from life in the South through some of the influences that I have already referred to and those that I will describe as the book progresses. And when I juxtapose my teenage interest in apartheid South Africa, civil rights US and the Vietnam War, it becomes apparent I knew more about far-away continents than the affairs of people and places only forty miles down the road. I am therefore very aware, and will never underestimate, the power of education and societal influence via community and media; in context of my own upbringing, I look upon such influences as being extremely limiting.

Valerie and I then holidayed in Connemara in 1976 and used the opportunity to visit some of Valerie's family circle in Ardrahan, south Galway. We became very regular visitors to their home while also using many weekends and subsequent summer holidays to visit different areas around Ireland. Through these visits and by increasingly following the Irish media, I began to see the socio-political structure of the country, noting it was a lot more complete when compared with the North as an appendage of London structures. And, of course, my increasing personal knowledge contrasted with the limited coverage northern media gave on the South. I never heard the good stories but when, for example, the 'recession' of the eighties happened and the numerous elections of that era occurred, northern media outlets were keen to carry the negative. The average Unionist, even if interested, would have received a very limited and value-laden diet. When one adds in those who were disinterested and downright hostile, it is clear that Unionist knowledge of the rest of Ireland was so limited it really was a testament to small-town isolationism. This mindset wasn't only limited to the 'ordinary working person', I tragically found that well-educated professionals were similarly conditioned and more interested in Downing Street than Dublin. However, my interest in *all* aspects of the island became the norm for me, and continued to increase when much later, we moved as a family to Dublin. Some of the issues that struck me were as follows.

I was in a position to learn of the decisive moves that Ireland was able to make down through its short history, such as its membership of the League of Nations, then the United Nations and the EEC/EU. The North, always as an appendage of Great Britain, could not make such decisions in its own right. One decision which I feel has given Ireland great credence as a small nation was in adopting a serious peacekeeping role, particularly in Africa and the Middle East. Ireland's reputation is enhanced by its army's service, whereas the British armed role has, in more recent times, led mostly to negative perceptions as one that has followed the US into highly questionable wars. That freedom to decide and carve out one's role in such organisations is for me an incredibly important right which Unionists have lost out on by only being a small part of the UK, hence having a very limited political role.

Readers will identify to some degree with the EU even if working knowledge of it is limited. Membership has had both very practical and symbolic benefits for Ireland. I met Dublin businesspeople who spoke of the importance of the British market but also spoke of 'leapfrogging' over Britain to Berlin to do European business. This confidence and pragmatism came from EU membership. For the country to be an equal member with the UK was highly symbolic given the very difficult nature of the relationship between the two nations. But the practical benefits were also immense, and a lot of those benefits came from the freedom the Dublin administration had in working the EU machine.

I met many of the Irish 'team' in Brussels via a European project I worked in with the University of Ulster, and then as a member of an NI Assembly and Business Sector study tour. The resources devoted to the Irish team and the actual work these people did to maximise benefits for Ireland was very impressive. They were in there networking and influencing to make sure Ireland's interests were protected. The North was the poor relation and northern businesspeople on the study tour recognised this. When one thinks that although there was 'peace money' available, the North did not benefit from the EU in the way the South did over decades. So something it seems was amiss in the Northern Irish approach. The weakness was very apparent: London civil servants looked after England's interests first and foremost, as the long fight for 'special status' for the North displayed. This was the EU categorisation that would render maximum benefits for Northern Ireland, but because the UK as a whole couldn't get such status it meant that London government priorities did not deliver for the North for a long time. The appropriate London government Minister didn't even attend important Brussels meetings on fish quotas for example, something that was very important to the North. Nowadays Ministers from Belfast attend, but I have to admit that I feel the Assembly has a very long way to go to maximise influence and benefits within and from the EU. During my time in the Assembly there was a report on improving their 'EU performance', but if they are only reporting at this stage they will take a long time playing catch up.

Ireland has, in 2012, taken up the chair of the 56-member-state Organisation for Security and Co-operation in Europe (OSCE) which is the world's largest regional security organisation. This is another example of the country punching above its weight as it leads that organisation in its human rights, conflict prevention and crisis management work in the incredibly important post 'Arab Spring' era. It is also another instance of something of standing and repute being open to an independent country.

These are only a few illustrations, and I will refer to others later in the book. I totally appreciate the sovereignty issues associated with the economy, which I believe will be eventually repaired, but suffice to say at the moment that Ireland had the freedom to establish its own positions on many crucial issues in stark contrast with Unionism that wanted to be integral to the UK but has had a very compromised integration. A semi-detached status has not served Unionism well. The central point is that Unionism loses out by being an appendage of London; that loss is about real political freedom and maturity.

I will now move to a more detailed look at the North.

Chapter Three

The North

My approach in this chapter is to convey a more particular type of examination of socio-political life in the North. I will draw on, but not exclusively restrict myself to, personal experiences and knowledge. I want to take this route as the thrust of the book is on a united Ireland and clearly one of the biggest changes required to achieve that end will be an adjustment in the position of people who presently regard themselves as Unionists. I will refer in detail, but again not exclusively, to that community because I was part of it and therefore in a position to have some insight. I want to use that personal insight as a base for my commentary, rather than deliver another conventional account of the history of the North since partition.

The separation of the six counties from the rest of Ireland became a sense of pride to most Unionists, but yet again irony raises its head. I would contend that the restricted population size, combined with the Unionist exclusivist desire to control politics and culture are, among other things, the real Achilles heel of the North. For example, if we take that early desire by Unionists to control the 'province'; Nationalist/Republican socio-political boycotts or the Nationalist community's sheer lack of identification with the North; the usual part of the population that was simply indifferent to political involvement; then it is clear that those taking positions in the various post-partition institutions came from a very limited political and civic gene pool. Despite being part of the Empire and the Commonwealth, the Northern Ireland political and public service community was, according to many, far too insular, short-sighted and defensive. Claims to be 'British' were not inclusive and expansive statements that reflected a genuine desire to be part of a multi-cultural entity; they were instead—in the opinion of many—statements of parochial control, superiority and anti-Irishness, posing under the guise of 'Britishness', that ultimately reinforced the oft-quoted and well-entrenched 'siege-mentality' of Ulster Unionists.

Central and local politics, the Protestant churches, police, civil service, media, crucial businesses and 'state' education became the preserve of mostly conservative operators shaped by separation tendencies inherent in partition. Unionists, instead of having the vision of winning over the incredibly small Nationalist population, scored massive own goals and created that particular 'factory of grievances'. If we now fast forward to the early twenty-first century and the period of centenary commemorations of so many special and important events in Irish history, including partition itself, then what have the Unionists got? They are now in a power-sharing Executive, with very limited powers, in which the major players are the DUP and Sinn Féin. The Deputy First Minister is an ex-IRA commander and there is a 'democratic stand-off' anchored in the Belfast Assembly. But before examining that in more detail, let me first deal with other issues. I refer here to local government, policing and media and in the following chapter I will deal with the all- important central government issues.

Local Government

I attended church as a small child and witnessed the Remembrance Sunday service into which the local Councillors paraded bedecked in their robes. My mother had a healthy disrespect for them and as I grew up I realised why. The standards, even of those who had important titles such as 'Captain' etc., were very poor, and a Unionist councillor I met in the early 1980s was, like many others, just a dreadful bigot. A Lurgan town clerk (a role now described as 'Chief Executive') whom I got to know later in life, was so poor intellectually, so totally conservative, and so narrow and Unionist in outlook it is no wonder local government got a bad image. Lurgan/Craigavon was the location for example, where die-hard Unionist councillors were eventually fined for their bias in dealing with a planning application by local GAA club, St Peter's, to obtain ground for their club headquarters. Seventeen councillors had to pay nearly a quarter of a million pounds damages to the GAA club for their "wilful misconduct" over an extended period. I knew one of those councillors and quite frankly he was one of those 'not a Fenian about the place' types. I know that term has been used as a hard-hitting cliché, but in this case it is accurate. If we then take the infamous chronicles of local councils with housing allocation and biased appointments based on religious labels, it is no wonder Nationalists/Republicans became alienated. The Derry area was particularly bad, and John Hume's portrayal of the situation there as a "microcosm of the Irish problem" and the "Achilles heel of the whole unionist-based Northern Ireland experiment" is a particularly pithy one (Hume's foreword to Frank Curran *Derry: Countdown to Disaster*, Gill and Macmillan 1986).

But if we think all the negatives of local government and politics were in the dim and distant past, we would be badly mistaken. I was elected as an SDLP councillor to Coleraine Borough Council in 2001 and was, because of my party activism, very well aware of the local politics even before that date. I then became the first ever elected Sinn Féin councillor to that council, subsequent to my move to that party. I once said that Coleraine would be one of the last bastions of narrow unionism/loyalism. My abiding memory of the town as my family moved to the area in 1993 was that of a loyalist attack on a house in the town. The reason was that a member of the family living there had appeared in a press photo celebrating Derry's all-Ireland GAA victory. In addition, and likely related, was the fact that one of the more progressive Unionist councillors had to abandon his plans to civically welcome, as Mayor, the Derry team and the 'Sam Maguire' trophy to Coleraine Borough Council. The reaction of the DUP was cynical. They urged the people of Coleraine to 'remain calm' despite such 'provocation'. The Mayor, David McClarty, received a phone call to his constituency office warning him that he would get a bullet in the head if he proceeded with the civic reception idea. His son who worked at a second constituency office received a similar call. These events typified the town to me.

Between that event and winning election to Coleraine Council, I was once again reminded of the strength of loyalist opinion and numbers in the town, and how the local police wouldn't take action. During one of the Orange Order Drumcree stand-offs in Portadown, Coleraine loyalists decided to flex their muscle by blocking roads. It is easy to cause chaos in Coleraine. They blocked the 'new bridge', and traffic was sent to cross the River Bann at the 'old bridge' in the middle of the town. By the time I got there one evening when trying to get home, the old bridge was also blocked by the loyalists. Police officers were actually stopping traffic before the bridge but within sight of the loyalists engaging in their illegal acts. When I asked what was going to be done, the police officer gave his pathetic reply that they didn't want to do anything. I, along with many others, had to travel many miles to cross the river at a point well removed from Coleraine.

As an elected councillor, I spoke out against the behaviour of a loyalist band and their supporters who held an impromptu, 'parade' in Coleraine after Glasgow Rangers had won an important football match. I received complaints that their behaviour was unacceptable as they were seen as intimidating people and were parading without the necessary permission. My home was promptly attacked by young men throwing a paint-bomb through a bedroom window and leaving a hoax bomb at the front door. It was clear that parts of local loyalism thought others shouldn't speak out against them.

However, the worst example from this Unionist-dominated area was the murder of Kevin McDaid in the Heights area of Coleraine in May 2009. Kevin was killed when a group of Loyalists with a long record of hatred against Nationalist/Republican people in a particular street, launched an attack. After a drink-filled session watching Rangers playing Celtic, a large number of the Rangers fans made their way to that street with their crude weapons. Kevin was attacked, knocked to the ground and killed. At the Council meeting three days later, the only mention was a brief statement of regret by the Unionist Mayor who appeared more concerned about moving on to the business agenda. A number of Unionist councillors who usually had plenty to say when negatives came from the Nationalist/Republican community, had very little to say about this disgusting killing and all that underpinned it. I immediately intervened, expressing my disappointment at the brevity and shortcomings of the mayoral statement, and requested a minute's silence as a mark of respect. The councillors had very little option but to accede to my request, even though reluctance may have been their real feeling. In addition, only two of the other 21 councillors attempted to pay their respects at the house, none of the Unionists attended the funeral and even First Minister Peter Robinson was being advised by local Unionists not to visit the McDaid home. However, to his credit he did visit, although I personally know that Deputy First Minister Martin McGuinness exerted considerable pressure on him to do so.

In the Office of the First Minister and Deputy First Minister (OFMDFM), subsequent meetings were held to deal with the sectarian troubles in Coleraine and other areas. Unfortunately, whilst Unionists, Alliance and most disappointingly SDLP councillors all spoke about law and order issues, and even referred to the relatively few Nationalist/Republican people who caused trouble in the Heights, they failed to address the fundamental hatred that bolstered the actions of the Loyalists.

At Council level, my time overlapped with what was described to me as the last of the generation of Unionist appointments; that is, those 'old boy' staff appointments made before equality and recruitment laws and procedures came into force. In context of the ethos and responsibilities of good public service, the standards of some of these people left a lot to be desired. I know that when I moved to Sinn Féin one junior supervisor instructed a member of staff under his control not to speak to me. I was informed of other staff members who would avoid contact with me whenever possible. However, I do acknowledge that senior staff treated me as they should – simply as another elected representative. Still, Coleraine Borough Council upheld its policy of flying the Union flag 365 days per year and constantly failed to recognise the negative message it conveyed to Irish people in the Borough. Worse still, two Chief Executives that overlapped with me failed to deal with an illegal Union flag permanently flying at a Council depot; they feared the reaction of the broader Unionist community.

Life with the councillors ranged from the comical to the dreadfully shallow. A couple of Unionist Councillors still wouldn't speak to me or have their photograph taken with me, even when I stood down in 2011. But the worst side of their parochial Unionism was revealed when it came to issues involving Irish culture, and this was not restricted to Ian Paisley's Democratic Unionists, some Ulster Unionists were just as bad. The difficulty that Unionists had delivering Council funding to help local GAA clubs establish new grounds or expand existing facilities, was intense. But subtle and not so subtle reminders by the Chief Executive, that the Council had a legal responsibility to provide the funds finally prevailed. Most Unionists abstained from voting on the matter, so that they were simultaneously seen by their backyard supporters as not supporting such funding, whilst avoiding a vote against that would leave them open to legal challenge.

The threat of legal action was again needed to convince Unionists to introduce a Coleraine Council policy facilitating street and road signs that included the Irish language. This was only successful after three to four years of delaying tactics by all the Unionists. After many meetings, rows and frustrations, a Barrister was eventually called in as the legal challenge came closer. So, with Unionist backs to the wall, the measure went through with Unionist abstentions again being their fail-safe. But most comical of all was the Democratic Unionist Mayor who refused to invite me (and subsequently some political colleagues) to an informal Christmas reception simply because I was in Sinn Féin. Despite advice from the Chief Executive the DUP Mayor insisted there would be no invitation. We simply challenged him by judicial review and attended the event anyway, and the Council was fined £10,000, which created massive Council embarrassment as the stupidity of the move gave the media a field day. The DUP then decided to pay the £10,000 so that the rate-payer did not, in effect, foot the bill: those were very expensive sausage-rolls!

I refer to these earlier and later events from local councils to illustrate the negative record of local government, much of which was underpinned by entrenched Unionist attitudes.

Policing

It is often said that society can be judged by its prisons. I can see the wisdom of that statement, particularly when one thinks of the Hunger Strikes and the profound commentary they provided on prisons and society at that incredibly difficult time. I would add that policing is also a good yardstick. I have already mentioned the significance of An Garda Síochána being formed in a political cauldron in the South and surviving to serve in a post-civil war society. The British 'bobby' has a long symbolic record and policing role, but differs considerably from the New York cop, who is also a product of his community. Likewise, the history of the RUC in the North also provides a commentary of sorts on Northern society. As I have already outlined, I have some experience of policing via six years of part-time membership of the RUC Reserve in Lurgan, a town which lost several police officers and had many injured by IRA actions. I therefore want to highlight some of my observations and experiences to continue this look at Unionism in the North.

It was common knowledge that the RUC, both full and part-time, were mainly recruited from the Unionist community. The full and part-time Ulster Defence Regiment (UDR) and the full-time Prison Service which grew exponentially in the 1970s certainly drank from the same recruitment well. Many will say it is totally understandable, but whether understandable or not, it certainly had a massive impact on the political-security outlook both prior to and during 'the Troubles'. Too many of the so-called 'leaders' of Northern society were afraid to look at solutions beyond their own community. I also believe there was a depressing failure to see beyond the security response for decades, before the penny finally dropped: this was a *political* problem requiring a *political* response.

For example, as we collectively moved towards the ceasefires of 1994, 'even the dogs on the street knew we were on that track' – as they say. But after an IRA attack, Ken Maginnis of the Ulster Unionists was calling for internment to be re-introduced! In the early 1980s and via my professional work I knew Bill Craig, former Unionist Home Affairs Minister. He was famous for alleging that the Civil Rights movement of the 1960s was a front for the IRA; as leader of Vanguard, a right-wing Unionist grouping, he spoke of "liquidating the enemy". When speaking one-to-one with him or in broader company, conversations invariably turned to politics. Bill Craig, even at that stage, could only see a security response. He spoke to me of the police "not wanting" to win the battle against the IRA. Despite prompts by me and others Craig did not, even once, articulate anything that approached a political vision, never mind see the need for a political solution; for him it was all about police and army "victories". Even earlier than that, I knew the senior police officer who was filmed infamously lashing out with his blackthorn stick at civil rights marchers in Derry in the late 1960s. That officer served in Lurgan before going to Derry, and undoubtedly he and others typified a generation of policing that couldn't see beyond a security response, something that was in my opinion totally inadequate for the context.

But there were worse examples than these, examples that displayed the fatal dangers of security forces identifying so totally with the state when the state is deeply polarised and in serious conflict. I will refer to some of these below but before doing so, and in the interest of balance, I want to refer to two RUC officers I knew personally, who became victims.

I joined the RUC Reserve in mid-to-late 1975. By that time 'the Troubles' were a daily reality that shaped everyone's lives. Police officers had already been killed in Lurgan; one of these was killed in an ambush on St Patrick's Day 1974. He was Constable Cyril Wilson who lived just one hundred yards from my family home and we would often see him leaving for work or coming home from duty. He was in a police Landover patrolling Craigavon, a so-called 'new city' that was to join Lurgan and neighbouring Portadown. The vehicle was fired on and Cyril Wilson, aged only 36, was killed. My mother woke me up the following morning with the news. She was obviously shocked and saddened, and I admit I was too. His death was in the melting pot of my thoughts when I then decided to join the force.

I could only describe Cyril Wilson as a gentleman, the community-type police officer. He would have been horrified by the wrongdoing of colleagues.

The second officer, Inspector Harry Cobb, was killed in an ambush at a security barrier in Church Place, Lurgan, at which vehicles were checked before entering the town. This site had already proved to be vulnerable as other attacks had been mounted on police officers there, including one who was killed. Harry Cobb had arrived to check the constables opening the barrier. They were all bunched together when IRA members came out of business premises hidden behind a large corrugated iron construction which was intended to protect the police.

I recall this particular incident for two reasons. Firstly, I too operated this barrier on many Saturday mornings. It was regarded as the most dangerous duty at 7am, but as a precaution I would stand back a considerable distance from the two other police officers when they approached the barrier to open it. I was armed and was giving cover to the two colleagues. I did this in order to be able to see the whole site and for precisely the reason that was exposed by Harry Cobb's murder. Officers walking together, not taking basic precautions was incredibly slack in my opinion and inexcusable, because Cobb was killed in February 1977, years into 'the Troubles', by which time many harsh lessons should have been well learned.

The second reason I recall this incident is because one of the gang who murdered Inspector Cobb was Leo Green. Leo was a member of a strong Republican family and lost his brother, John Francis (1975), also an IRA member, at the hands of loyalist gunmen who were always thought to be acting in collusion with security forces. He later took part in the Hunger Strikes and much later worked in the Stormont Assembly as one of the key Sinn Féin staffers. I worked with him, but understandably we never spoke about any aspect of the Harry Cobb murder or anything of his IRA past. But it is feasible that Green and his associates might have been launching an attack on me at that Lurgan security barrier. Even by Irish standards this little circle of former part-time policeman and former IRA man working in power-sharing Stormont thirty years later is, to say the least, an interesting one.

But apart from that little aside, Harry Cobb, like Cyril Wilson, would not have approved of the maverick security personnel. I had knowledge of that group as well.

After the 1974 Ulster Workers' Council strike and the Dublin-Monaghan bombings, rumours abounded that some in the security forces were involved with loyalist paramilitaries. There was much talk of the Ulster Defence Regiment being actively involved, especially when an earlier arms raid on a Lurgan UDR base was cynically described as a 'break-out'. This arose from local, on-the-street knowledge that some of the gang stealing the weapons were actually serving UDR members from that base.

But in and around the time I was applying for and starting with the RUC Reserve, one of the most notorious massacres of 'the Troubles' occurred. This was the killing of members of the Miami Showband, one of Ireland's top musical bands. They had been playing in Banbridge, only nine miles from my hometown, and were stopped by a UVF gang masquerading as an official British Army checkpoint as the band left Banbridge heading south to Newry and over the border. Efforts by the gang to place a bomb inside the band's vehicle went wrong. It exploded prematurely, killing two of the gang, whose colleagues then opened fire on the bandsmen they had lined up at the side of the road. Three band members were killed, two injured and the incident is still regarded as one of the worst of 'the Troubles'.

It has been alleged by former MI6 agent, Fred Holroyd, that the killings were organised by British Army officer Robert Nairac, something doubted by Martin Dillon, author of *The Dirty War*. Nairac was himself later killed by the IRA when he was kidnapped outside a South Armagh pub which he visited under the guise of a Republican supporter. Nairac was working with Robin Jackson, often called 'the Jackal', an infamous Lurgan man who commanded the Mid-Ulster UVF and who conveniently left the Ulster Defence Regiment after the 'break-out' described above. I then found it very surprising, when writing this book, that families of the Miami band members killed and injured were themselves surprised that Jackson would be classed in a report by the Historical Enquiries Team as, 'an agent of the RUC'. It was dog-on-the-street knowledge that Jackson was also an RUC agent. The families disclosed that the report even indicated Jackson was tipped off by police officers that his fingerprints were found on tape on the silencer of a gun used in the incident. But, on the bigger picture of Jackson's work with RUC handlers, the report also said that two officers who could have shed light on these issues were Detective Superintendent Drew and Detective Chief Inspector Murray (*Irish Times* 15 Dec. 2011). I remember Frank Murray, who was later seriously injured in an IRA attack in Lurgan. His 'driven' recuperation from the horrific injuries and return to police work was highly respected amongst police officers, but there appears to be no doubt that Frank Murray was deeply involved in the 'special' forces of his RUC and the British Army, many times working with loyalist paramilitaries.

But for me there was an interesting and illuminating footnote to Frank Murray's story. I interviewed Ken Maginnis in March 1996 while he was still the Ulster Unionist MP for Fermanagh South Tyrone. The interview was for my doctoral research, but in the general conversation I told Maginnis I was originally from Lurgan, and he immediately identified the town with Frank Murray. The MP then told me that he had been able to use his influence to get Murray on to the Queen's Honours list before he died. Maginnis took great pleasure in Murray being a Catholic police officer who did so much against the IRA and then accepted a Queen's Honour. I personally had an alternative view: the establishment rewards—with that aura of societal respectability—those who work with loyalist terrorists in a 'dirty war'.

It also transpired that one of the UVF Miami murder gang was a former British soldier, and a further two of the UVF men were serving members of the UDR. I knew both of the UDR men and their families and heard a lot of the local talk in the Unionist community immediately after the murders. This experience once again demonstrated how many of that community could be absolutely withering in their reaction to republican killings but prevaricated when it came to loyalist killings.

Interestingly, one of those UDR/UVF men was also a member of the same Orange Lodge I belonged to briefly. I was at a monthly Lodge meeting when a letter of resignation from him was read out: he resigned immediately after being arrested to avoid the embarrassment of being described as an Orangeman involved in murder. The fudging by other Orangemen in the room that night on the gravity of this man's violence was illuminating; there wasn't one negative word. One man, another part-time policeman, even said that because guilt wasn't proved the Lodge should not accept his resignation. However, others were a little wiser and more pragmatic, realising it was better that he wasn't connected with the Lodge when it came to media coverage of the court appearances.

The name Robin Jackson would come up many times as Lurgan was part of the infamous 'murder triangle', an area in which it is estimated that fifty people were killed in the second half of 1975. The UVF was instrumental in many of these killings and often their victims were chosen solely because of their religion. The O'Dowd family, who lost three members when their home in Ballydougan, between Lurgan and Gilford, was attacked by the UVF in January 1976, were quite well known to me because some of my wife's family were very friendly with them. Later in life I would also work with one of that family circle in the Belfast Assembly. This was John O'Dowd who became Minister for Education in the North in May 2011. It is reckoned that the O'Dowd murders and those of the Reavey family in South Armagh on the same night led to the murder of ten Protestants by the IRA the following evening in Kingsmill, also in County Armagh. This was the era of 'tit for tat' killings.

It later turned out that the local UVF had contacts beyond the UDR. Two RUC officers, whom I knew when they served in Lurgan, were charged in the late seventies with terrorist offences, Constable Billy McCaughey with murder and kidnap and Sergeant Gary Armstrong with kidnap. The kidnap victim was Roman Catholic priest, Father Hugh Murphy, taken in retaliation for an IRA kidnapping and murder of an RUC officer. Billy McCaughey served time in prison, later becoming a public figure in the Progressive Unionist Party (PUP), the political voice of the UVF. The extent of RUC and UDR members' involvement in terrorism is much more public now. Judge Barron's 2003 investigation into the Dublin and Monaghan bombings has made very serious links between people and incidents through the weapons used in various attacks. It is clear that this was more than a few rotten apples. Barron names Armstrong as one of a group of RUC men who carried out a gun and bomb attack on the Rock Bar near Keady, Co. Armagh, in June 1976. Throughout this period, UVF commander Robin Jackson lived a 'charmed' life avoiding serious investigation. An RUC officer once told a court hearing a murder case that Jackson was not before the court as part of an "operational strategy".

The arrest of McCaughey and Armstrong was a wake-up call for me, still only in my early twenties. The rumours of collusion were true: a part of the 'legal force' included officers killing and bombing, yet still claiming to be on the higher moral ground. The silence of police officers and large swathes of unionism on these issues was deafening. I had a friendly debate with my mother on the day that news of McCaughey and Armstrong broke, essentially saying that policing could never be like this and would have to radically change. I am not claiming to have foreseen the Patten changes of 1999, but I knew that if policing change didn't happen ultimately the bigger political changes would likewise not happen. My mother's reaction was that changes in policing would "never take place". Such a reaction is illuminating in itself: my mother was an educated lady, knowledgeable in her history, but couldn't see how change of this nature could possibly happen in such a society.

Another reaction of my mother's was similarly illuminating. Years later, as I researched my doctorate on state and paramilitary violence, I asked her about one of these UDR/UVF people involved with Jackson, McCaughey, and Armstrong. This was Robert McConnell, whose family circle would have been known to my mother's family circle in her original South Armagh home area. It is now understood that McConnell was 'run' by RUC Special Branch and Military intelligence, particularly Robert Nairac, and was involved in many murders including the Dublin and Monaghan bombings, as well as being integral to the 'Glenanne gang', a name given to the UVF in that general area and beyond. My mother didn't think it was possible that Robert McConnell was involved with the UVF. This kind of disbelief was common. People steeped in the 'law and order' tradition find it hard to believe that the 'dirty war' was so dirty and that it really was the likes of the RUC/UDR neighbour that took part in it. They perhaps internalise a belief system which finds all this hard to accept: it is another 'mental ceiling'. For example, many Unionists I know still find it hard to accept what is now the official version of Bloody Sunday, that the dirty war was very real and not just Republican propaganda. They continue to mentally block out the disturbing implications of security forces that do their community's fighting by foul means.

In deep contrast, those who fought the state—(and let's remember it was the IRA who eventually killed Robert McConnell in April 1976)—the 'dirty war' was integral to 'the Troubles' and for many, including the families who have lobbied and campaigned on this issue, this is a tragic but very straightforward truth. The state, it seems, can 'fight dirty' and use local supporters who are willing to help. This has happened in many conflicts in which the British have been a player, as testified to by British General Frank Kitson, who wrote on this subject using his experiences in Malaya, Kenya and the North.

But the difficulties of bad policing were not restricted to security force members double-jobbing in the paramilitary groups. The policy of 'Ulsterisation' adopted by the British Government from the late seventies brought the RUC into the primary security role. This led to numerous controversial incidents, one of which was the November 1982 killing of three unarmed IRA men shot in their car by RUC officers in Craigavon. Within two weeks a young man was killed by an undercover RUC team in nearby Lurgan. These were two of a cluster of deadly clashes which became known as the 'shoot-to-kill' incidents.

The attitude among police officers I knew was that the victims got what they deserved and the police were now taking them on. But difficulties with the police versions of events, including admitted lies by RUC officers at failed trials, resulted in the famous Stalker inquiry. John Stalker was Deputy Chief Constable of Greater Manchester Constabulary and was appointed to investigate the killings. Knowledge on the Lurgan street was that Stalker had visited families of the killed, assuring them he would get to the bottom of the cases. After I had left the RUC Reserve I met a relatively young Constable who was to be interviewed by Stalker. I don't know the nature of his involvement. The Constable laughed at the idea of the interview, saying that Stalker would get no help from him and that in terms of the overall inquiry "the Brit would get nowhere".

Later, after Stalker had submitted his interim report with recommendations for prosecutions of RUC officers and posing serious questions about police and political leadership, he was removed from the inquiry over his alleged links with a Manchester criminal. The political dirty tricks had won. I had heard that some within the families of the victims told Stalker he would never get to the bottom of the cases, and that his British colleagues would not allow him to do his job if it created problems for them. It was clear they were correct. Stalker was later to write about the dirty tricks campaign and how he had been obstructed by RUC members from the Chief Constable, Jack Hermon, down. (*Stalker*, Harrap, 1988, 262-271).

Media Influence

I am one of those people with deep respect for the role of media in society. My yardsticks are Walter Lippman, John Pilger, Robert Fisk and Al Jazeera. However, I still have a healthy questioning attitude towards the media. When I hear of *Fox News* in the US speaking of its objective reporting I have to laugh for a moment. And when I translate that into the local scenario I wonder which is the more 'objective', is it the *Irish News* or the *News Letter*, similarly the *Irish Times* or the *Irish Independent*, and indeed *RTÉ* or *BBC NI*? But I think it is important when looking at the Unionist experience in the North to briefly mention the media's influence; in part that influence has been a malign one.

The written media were obviously the news outlet in the immediate aftermath of partition. But, down through the decades, radio and TV became additional norms with their shaping influences, something we should not underestimate. Eamonn De Valera was a very particular Irish example of someone who realised the power of a printed medium reflecting his outlook when the *Irish Press* was launched in 1931, and we must accept that on a broader scale and in more recent times Silvio Berlusconi and Rupert Murdoch similarly know the influence the media can have on people and society.

Unionists in the North had their own papers which largely reflected their views, whilst the leading management and movers in radio and TV were also Unionists. BBC Radio Ulster and its predecessors, UTV and BBCNI, were largely Unionist or, using the most benign description, 'unionist-leaning'. In addition, both the local BBC and UTV were part of large British media organisations which actually provided the vast majority of programming and international news. The 'back to Jeremy in London' syndrome epitomises how anchored in the British worldview much of the Northern media is. BBC Northern Ireland constantly introduces some 90% of its programmes that are basically British. Its own local news is the tail-end news because it is dominated by GB news and values. It is pervasive. I have often challenged people to temporarily change their media diet from British to Irish, and in more recent times even to Al Jezeera, just to test for themselves how views are shaped. I suspect there haven't been too many unionist-minded people taking up the challenge and temporarily deserting the *News Letter*/*BBC*/ *UTV* axis. In short, much of the media diet would appear to be dominated by a Unionist and British outlook. Reflections of Irishness were, if not missing altogether, certainly minimal and mostly negative. As a self-confessed 'news junkie', and with the exception of the *Irish News* I struggled to get feedback about southern society via northern TV, Radio and written media. So for the average Unionist it was a case of almost total immersion in a little Northern bubble; and if they didn't listen or watch predominantly 'mainland' news their worldview was an even smaller one. This domination wasn't even broken with the coming of the internet era.

Unionists did not like the thought of the Dublin authorities expanding their media services into the North, realising that this would have a cultural influence: it follows therefore that the cultural and political influence of Unionist-and-British was a purposeful enterprise, solidifying their sense of identity and aspirations. I once attended a BBC briefing in Belfast for elected representatives at which I complained about their lack of news about the rest of Ireland which, I argued, would be appreciated by those with an Irish identity in the North. Essentially I did not get an answer. I later raised the same point with the BBC Governor Fabian Monds at one of their road-show meetings in Portstewart. Again I was apparently wasting time and breath.

Some media outlets would not even report on Gaelic games. It was the 1990s before local TV stations showed some GAA matches, but of course the only time you heard of Kerry was when they played Derry. In effect, twenty-six of the GAA counties did not exist in media terms, except when playing one of the six northern counties. When the Irish rugby team selection was made for example, BBC reporters many times *only* referred to northern players. This, and practices like it, are excruciatingly embarrassing.

So on the serious socio-political front there is no doubt that British/Unionist leanings supported by a British/Unionist dominated media had a big shaping influence in the North. Overall the media constantly reinforced that worldview. The Northern media did not challenge the difficult pre-troubles issues of housing allocations and unjust employment practices, and during 'the Troubles' many outlets failed to expose collusion, state violence and corruption. When loyalists torched whole Belfast streets in August 1969, the BBC were somehow able to cover the event without reference to the source of the attacks! Martin Bell, who later became a senior BBC reporter (and then a British Member of Parliament), was part of the BBC team in Belfast at the time and admitted some eight years later that this was a mistake. He said this was the only time he was stopped by superiors from saying what he wanted to say (John Horgan, *Irish Media: A Critical History Since 1922*, Routledge, 2001).

Local and GB coverage of, for example, 'Bloody Sunday' was lamentable, and the role of BBC World Service following that fateful day was to get British Army and Government propaganda out to the international community as effectively as possible. The local BBC described many early to mid-seventies murders carried out by loyalist paramilitaries as mere 'motiveless killings'; but many of these were in the murder triangle and involved the RUC and UDR members mentioned earlier in this chapter. So not only did the media fail to call them as they were, that is, sectarian killings, but they also failed to investigate the many claims of collusion. These failings further reinforced an unquestioning attitude towards the media, among many unionist-minded people.

In addition, and at an important socio-cultural level, much of the Northern media restricts itself to the geography of Northern Ireland. While there have been some improvements lately, there has undoubtedly been a long-term very narrow and parochial diet. This ensured isolation from the South and assured a lack of appreciation for much of Irish culture and life, even among people regarding themselves as Irish. Again, being Irish in the North was a compromised identity.

I will now move on to deal with the crucial and difficult issues of central government in N Ireland in the next chapter.

Chapter Four

Government in N Ireland:
Absolute Power To Democratic Deficit

The new Belfast government/administration set about its work in the 1920s, reflecting the ethos of 'a Protestant parliament for a Protestant people' in its deeds. On the security front there was an immediate move to establish the Ulster Special Constabulary (USC) along the lines of the UVF. Its full-and part-time classes were virtually exclusively Protestant/Unionist, so the seeds of a police force for one section of the community, and for the state's biased protection, were immediately and firmly sewn. Sections of the USC were extremely undisciplined, and the 'B' section secured their largely sectarian place in history by their ruthless suppression of the Catholic/Nationalist /Republican community. These 'B Specials' were notorious even down to my day and were eventually disbanded following the *Hunt Report* of 1969.

When I joined the RUC Reserve, some ex 'B' men already served in the Reserve. On a few occasions they lamented the passing of the 'B Specials' and their main claim was that, had the 'B's' still been in place, they would have dealt with the IRA. They also heavily hinted that they would have acted in a harsher direct way against Catholics and some of them even spoke in favourable terms of loyalist paramilitaries, who they saw as fighting for their country. But it wasn't only ex 'B' men who held this opinion. One Reservist spoke to me in categorical terms that if loyalist paramilitaries carrying a bomb were stopped at 'his' police checkpoint he would definitely allow them through.

But as well as the actual forces at their disposal, the Government also utilised the *Special Powers Acts*, which moved from annual renewal in the 1920s to five-year periods and then to permanency. When allied to a Unionist judiciary, Unionist-dominated juries by virtue of the property rule, and Unionists in the vast majority of senior Civil Service posts, it is easy to see that virtually the entire state apparatus was of one ilk with one overall ethos, that is, protecting the Unionist position. Paddy Hillyard was surely correct when he describes the law and order approach by successive Unionist governments as "highly repressive, sectarian and centralised" ('Law and Order' in *Northern Ireland: The Background to the Conflict* ed., John Darby, 1983, 35). There were also sectarian troubles throughout the 1920s, 30s and an IRA border campaign from 1956 to 1962, so trouble was never far away.

Employment was also an incredibly important issue: there was widespread exclusion of the Catholic/Nationalist/Republican community from many sectors. The worst manifestation of this was the 1931 Ulster Protestant League which encouraged Protestants to employ fellow Protestants, an approach endorsed by Basil Brooke as the Minister of Agriculture, who later became Prime Minister and Lord Brookeborough. But even when you got a job there might be difficulties. I remember a part-time RUC Reserve colleague telling me how he got the worst jobs in the Belfast dockyards because his name sounded 'catholic', until he wore a Masonic ring to work; suddenly he got the best jobs and even overtime.

But returning to Basil Brooke, I would consider him as the epitome of that narrow Unionist psyche and even some unionist-minded people would later admit to me that he had a major responsibility for the circumstances that led to conflict. My mother related a story of him going to Orange Hall meetings at election time. When he left one such meeting, he cynically said to his driver words to the effect 'just beat the drum and keep them happy'. In other words the votes would come from those Orange supporters as long as the 'Union drum' was beaten. There was absolutely no recognition of anything beyond that next election victory rendered by parochial, drum-beating tribalism.

There were always exceptions to general trends. However, many of the jobs in the major industrial companies, public service, broadcasting and the small business sector were controlled by Unionists, thus largely excluding Nationalists/Republican or, at least debarring them from senior positions. Books and other studies are replete with examples and statistics of how bad the situation was in the North during the first four decades of its existence. Of course there were ebbs and flows of market conditions such as in the 1930s depression years when many of the North's heavy industries suffered greatly. In contrast the expansion of international companies in the early 1960s gave Nationalists and Republicans better chances of gaining work from employers uninterested in sectarian recruitment approaches unless the Personnel Departments (now Human Resources) were headed by local Unionist-minded people!

The net result of these examples and others was that the Unionist-led central government was a discredited political animal. Even when the Prime Minister of Northern Ireland the more liberal Terence O'Neill met with the South's Taoiseach Seán Lemass in 1965, the hardliners soon created trouble for him, ultimately leading to perennial leadership problems as each Unionist leader looked over his shoulder for the next hard-liner. So, as the Civil Rights movement gained strength in the mid to late 1960s, a discredited Unionist government could not initially see the need to make the necessary changes. They protected their monolith at all costs, continued with their 'law and order' approach, and made more difficulties and indeed more enemies because of the way they treated Civil Rights marchers, and eventually lost control. Draconian measures such as the disastrous 1971 one-sided internment programme only heaped more trouble on the conflict and led to the watershed tragedy that was Bloody Sunday in January 1972. As well as tragically giving Derry families and the community fourteen physical coffins, it was in essence the final nail in the Ulster Unionist coffin.

Ulster Unionist central government was totally disgraced, and prorogued in March 1972 to be replaced by Direct Rule from London. It was clear even to me as a teenager that this type of administration could never return.

Before moving to the next part of my examination, I feel there is value in recording some reactions to Bloody Sunday in the week following the tragedy. By the following weekend I was in a group consisting of some fellow teenagers, some others in their early twenties who were either studying or had commenced work, and a young qualified teacher. All were Protestants of various denominations. By this stage Bloody Sunday had dominated the news, and the funerals of the victims had taken place, so it certainly wasn't a case of raw initial reaction. Most of the group I was with simply would not believe that the British Army had killed innocent civilians; there were numerous accounts of 'lies' from Nationalists/Republicans, therefore it followed that any Bloody Sunday stories from Derry Nationalists/Republicans were also lies. Accounts put out by the British Army, local and GB media that the Army was fired on, possibly by hundreds of rounds, were firmly believed and I really do stress firmly! But worst of all was the definite nature of the following 'fact' from Bloody Sunday: the young teacher told us authoritatively that bodies from previous shootings had been dragged out on to the Derry streets to make the whole event look worse; that some of the 'bodies' were even brought overnight from Donegal. Bizarre propaganda such as this in conflict situations crosses a mad line, but as long as people can retain the credibility of their tribe, the unbelievable quickly becomes very believable!

Present-day Central Government

Direct rule became a long-term position interspersed with various attempts to convene a locally-accountable administration in the North. The most notable was the 1973 Northern Ireland Assembly but, when it came to the Council of Ireland proposals in the December 1973 Sunningdale Agreement, trouble loomed: the UWC strike ensured 'the agreement' only lasted until 28 May 1974. The 1985 Anglo-Irish Agreement was clearly a very important landmark, but it wasn't until the structures established in the Good Friday Agreement became firmly rooted – and that was only in the third Belfast Assembly, in which I served – that we could say the North had a relatively settled local administration. This was the first local Assembly to survive a full-term. I would therefore like to give some personal reflection on the Assembly operation from my time there and from my general knowledge.

I served as MLA (Member of the Legislative Assembly) for the East Derry constituency, which has both strong Unionist and Nationalist/Republican areas, and which blends medium-sized towns, villages, swathes of rural farmland and coastal areas. East Derry also includes the Coleraine area in which I served as a Borough Councillor for 10 years and have referred to earlier.

There is a committee system at the Northern Ireland Assembly which has the legal responsibility to monitor each government ministry. Each committee is all-party in nature with numbers shaped by party strength. I was appointed by Sinn Féin to the Culture, Arts and Leisure (CAL) Committee; the Culture Arts and Leisure Minister at that time was the DUP's Nelson McCausland. I was also appointed to the Regional Development (RD) Committee; the corresponding Minister was Sinn Féin's Conor Murphy. Having one committee with a DUP Minister and the other from Sinn Féin often meant different approaches. Each committee met weekly so this part of the MLA's work is regular and could be substantial. The committee work is not generally well known, although it perhaps came to greater prominence during the third Assembly when some so-called controversial topics arose, and ministers had to attend to give account of their department's work.

In addition to committee work, I had to carry out the appropriate duties in the plenary sessions, for example, at question time or when a relevant CAL or RD subject was debated or a ministerial statement delivered.

There was a sense of achievement that the third Assembly did go the full term which, given the history of Belfast administrations, is understandable. I believe quite a lot of good work goes on in the committee system. Members will generally take their monitoring role seriously; can and have proposed sensible changes to legislation coming before them; will do a bit less grand-standing; but will also still play a party role, particularly when committee members want to score points against a minister from another party. But unfortunately, all these relative positives are many times countered by the politics of the ethno-political divide.

For example, when it came to debate about the Irish Language Act in plenary, or when the Minister came before the CAL committee, it was a very poor time for the Assembly. The worst I recall was a plenary session where I had the 'privilege' of summing up for Sinn Féin. Barry McElduff MLA and Gerry Adams, then MLA, were among the other SF speakers while Gregory Campbell MLA and Minister McCausland were among the DUP's. I can honestly say it was dismal; the level of Unionist debate was particularly low. So much so that I referred to Campbell's contribution as "a race to the bottom", and to be frank that was a pleasant way of describing it. When one of his DUP colleagues wanted to cut into my summation I, exceptionally, refused to allow him; I explained I couldn't take another minute of the mediocrity. It was that bad!

Nelson McCausland even played 'the long game' on a draft policy on minority languages, thereby delaying the process to the point of his departure from office in May 2011, without introducing it. Likewise when it came to McCausland's proposals for events that could mark the very important decade of commemorations of events from 1912-22, he somehow managed to leave out the 1916 rising. Always, when challenged about this, he would give his 'single transferable rant' about how 'little happened in Northern Ireland at that time'. The slight historical subtlety that Northern Ireland didn't exist 'at that time' eluded Mr McCausland for a while. When reminded about this he changed his reference to Ulster.

I fully appreciate that many readers will rank the Irish Language Act and the decade of commemorations against the needs for jobs, education and health provision, regarding the latter issues as more important on a daily-needs basis. I generally agree, and continue to try to put these into proper political and social perspective. However, despite being one of the smaller-spending departments, the work of Culture Arts and Leisure is a frontline area where concerns about diversity and acceptance of identities should be catered for. That frontline can be positive, or it can descend to a battle line. As one who has written a report on the management of diversity by government, and has been politically active on these very issues, I have to admit that the cultural situation in the North remains more of a battle line. I know that many people will be pleased to know that at least these issues are being debated in an assembly, and that the more politicians work together things might improve, but I am referring to something deeper than that.

It goes back to question of identity and allegiance. I am still far from convinced that being Irish in the North is adequately supported by the Assembly. At the most basic level—and I stress *most* basic—St Patrick's Day isn't even a public holiday. When this was debated in the Assembly it made absolutely no difference: a lame excuse came back from the Secretary of State. All of this of course contrasts with the main Orange day of celebration, the 12th July, being a public holiday. The abiding and overwhelming corporate identity of the North is British, through the marking of significant events, media, community and professional groups' links to GB rather than Ireland, and continuing cultural isolation from Ireland helps to maintain this. So, the provisions for identity-equality in the Good Friday Agreement have become an ongoing battle in which the status-quo and constitutionality—that largely serves the interests of Unionism—have a distinct advantage. While the popular attitude is to accept that things have 'moved on', I believe managing the diversity of identity and allegiances in the North has yet to be seriously addressed. Another example is the limited support and coverage of those few 'all-Ireland' bodies. So, even the promising dimension of an all-Ireland outlook is minimal, perhaps even non-existent, in the minds of the Irish community in the North, more than a decade after the Good Friday Agreement was signed.

Generally, I think the Assembly's overall quality of debate and the vision of many of the Assembly members is limited. I do not want to over-criticise, but the reaction of too many members of the public is negative. I know some people who went to Stormont to lobby for an issue and then took time to listen to some debates. With very few exceptions the verdict has been seriously critical, and letters in local papers have reflected that. I have to say that having followed events in the Assembly, and then having worked there, I have sometimes been astounded by the low quality of debate and poor grasp of the issues. With such limited powers and vision the Assembly certainly doesn't inspire my expectations for major advances. When I asked questions in the Assembly about attracting jobs and increasing tourism, responses were far from satisfactory. The abject failure of Unionist members and Ministers to really look at sensible all-Ireland approaches in, for example, tourism, was depressing. Constantly referring to 'Northern Ireland', caring only about 'Northern Ireland', and failing to recognise that such parochialism was restricting growth were regular faults even with the new 'Tourism Ireland' in existence. I appreciate the roles prescribed for Tourism Ireland and the NI Tourist Board, but there is a vast, untapped potential that I believe is seriously hindered by the politicised motivation of Unionism.

For example, the NI Tourist Board, local Councils, a Minister and Departmental officials worked on the promotion of a special tourist route (along the lines of the 'Ring of Kerry' idea) to increase visitor numbers to Ulster, and said that it finished at Magilligan, County Derry. At that time there was already an onward ferry from Magilligan to Greencastle in County Donegal. Given that the declared objective of the NI Tourist Board is to promote tourism 'in cooperation with Fáilte Ireland' (the tourist body in the South), one can only conclude that the six-county vision is more important to the unionist mind-set of many of those involved, rather than sensible tourism planning and marketing.

The following example is even more illuminating and worrying. *WikiLeaks* and the *Irish Independent* (7 June 2011) have provided an insight into the moving of 5000 financial services jobs from Dublin to Belfast. The fear was that Ireland would lose the jobs to Poland. Therefore it was deemed better for Dublin to lose them to Belfast as at least they would stay on the island.

Incredibly, we now know via a communication by the US Ambassador to Ireland, Tom Foley, to his Washington counterparts, that 'concerns were expressed' by some Stormont officials in Belfast about these jobs coming North from Dublin as there were "significant pockets of unionism that see stronger links with the South as an end-run to subjugate unionist communities in the North." That sort of old style 'papal plot' mind-set is so paranoid and/or confined to six-county thinking as to be virtually unbelievable and further shows there are still many people in relatively important public service positions whose restricted vision has to be overcome.

I want to finish this chapter by taking a broader look at where political Unionism is in the context of the Belfast Assembly. Unionism has come from 'their own parliament' to the structures of the Good Friday Agreement. If Unionist Prime Minister, J M Andrews, can declare in 1942 that a Unionist government in Northern Ireland must *always* be in power, it is clear that Unionism has moved from domination to power-sharing, and from being a monolith to having some serious fractures. In 2012, the DUP is by far the strongest Unionist party, something born out of pragmatism rather than any entrenched ideology; it has usurped the Ulster Unionist position, leaving a working-class unionist constituency that is not well represented. That demographic block had at least the early work of the Ulster Democratic Party (UDP), the political wing of the UDA and the better-known Progressive Unionist Party (PUP) from UVF lineage, but neither sustained electoral success. Because the DUP stance on issues such as education and jobs and skills training is so lamentably bad for people in working-class unionist heartlands I believe this part of society will not benefit much from a local assembly. In short, Unionism is now at the political point of merely maximising the power of the DUP over the Ulster Unionists, but the amount of that power is incredibly limited.

The Belfast Assembly has devolved powers, meaning there are two categories which it can't legislate on: firstly, 'reserved' matters, which are those that *could* be transferred to Belfast from the UK Parliament but presently, are not; and secondly, 'excepted' matters, which will always remain in London. Even if reserved matters were transferred to Belfast, the Assembly would still have a very limited remit. The net result means Unionism is—between power-sharing mechanisms and limited powers—at a very different place from where it first intended itself to be.

The Assembly doesn't have control of, for example, benefits, taxation, minimum wage, financial services, monopolies and mergers, civil defence, international relations (including being the poor relation in the UK's dealings with the EU), immigration, many aspects of security, land and buildings owned by the Crown, many aspects of sea-related activities and resources, and civil aviation. If I were to laboriously list all the legislative items that the Assembly *doesn't* have control over it could continue for a couple of pages! Suffice to say the Assembly is limited: one could cynically describe it as a glorified local council.

This is all graphically summed up when it comes to talking about the NI economy. In the truest sense, it doesn't really have an economy. The Assembly cannot even keep the tax revenue raised in the North; it goes to London. And whenever there is debate in the Assembly about raising revenue, the road-block of governance from London comes into play. Even within my short time in the Assembly the Minister of Finance said many times that if the North raised tax from whatever idea was being debated it would be of no net benefit to the North; whatever was raised would be deducted from the block grant, that is, deducted from the annual amount of money sent by London for the support of the North. In short, even Unionism is not anywhere near in control of its own financial future: it is part of an administration that merely receives an amount of money, and then divides it up between departments.

One of the best-known examples of financial issues which reveal the highly-restricted nature of the NI Assembly is that of Corporation Tax. At the time of writing, the desire to reduce Corporation Tax in the North to match the much lower and advantageous rate in the Republic still hasn't materialised. If this were to happen, the North would obviously have a rate considerably different from GB. But as this was raised *ad nauseum* by some MLAs for press-release and profile purposes, the Minister of Finance warned that if less Corporation Tax was taken in the North then this could have negative effects on the London block grant. His worries are extremely understandable when placed against remarks by British PM David Cameron on a visit to the Belfast Assembly on June 9th, 2011. Basically he declared support for a tax rate reduction in principle, but gave a warning that the days of dealing with any economic woe in the North by simply asking London for more money were over. Not so diplomatically perhaps, he reminded MLAs that the North received 25% more per head for its public services than other UK citizens.

The core of the difficulty is clear but stark. If the Corporation Tax rate in the North was cut from 25% to 12.5% (equivalent to the Republic's rate) the immediate knock-on effect would be £300+ million less tax intake. In which case, how would the Northern economy generate that shortfall immediately, and then for perhaps a decade, this being the minimum time it would take to bring Corporation Tax returns back up by attracting more businesses which pay the reduced tax rate? The weakness of this lower tax-rate proposition was recognised by the DUP Finance Minister Sammy Wilson who warned that actions to lower the Corporation Tax rate must not be "debilitating" to the NI economy (*Irish Times* 15 June 2011). The conundrum of the straightjacket finance system that is the block grant, is embodied in this issue. Take one understandable step forward but you automatically take one backwards. And, as an *Irish Times* editorial (28 March 2011) wisely noted, not only is it a financial issue but it is also "of some constitutional importance".

In short the Assembly's extremely limited role is crystal clear when it comes to matters of real substance. The occasional argument Unionists put up against my point of limited devolved powers is that Northern Ireland MPs at Westminster have input on all other important issues. This thesis is more rarely heard these days, because the general population know that the power exercised by the North's MPs is very limited indeed.

At this point therefore, it is clear that 90 years after exercising absolute power, all the Unionists have is a democratic deficit. They have little voice at Westminster, are part of a system in Belfast which has very limited powers and which I described earlier as a 'democratic stand-off'; even Unionists themselves recognise it as far from being a normal democracy. That abnormality leads directly from the abnormalities that underpinned partition, which were in turn administered by now-discredited Unionist administrations.

Chapter Five

Identity

The Irish actress Brenda Fricker wryly commented that if you're lying drunk in an airport you were Irish, but if you won an Oscar you were British. She was speaking in context of her own splendid 1989 Oscar victory when many in the British press claimed her as one of their own. Irish people in general are well used to this, and readers will I am sure have their own examples. For Northerners that Irish-British dialectic has an even more abrasive rub. It goes to the heart of identity in a society with profound socio-ethnic divisions that were considerably deepened by 'the Troubles' and then eased somewhat in the 'peace process'. However, I do not think we should rest easy trying to convince ourselves that everybody is doing their best to be good little 'Northern Irelanders' in a completed process. Therefore, I feel that I have to firmly deal with a related issue very early in this chapter.

Claiming to be a proud Irish person (or indeed a proud British person) in Northern Ireland is not necessarily narrow or excessively nationalistic. In addition having a singular Irish identity, should not be considered intellectually second-class when compared with some who claim—as is their right— to have a dual British/Irish identity. Again I refer to my self-description as 'a very contented Irishman' and I stress, yet again, this is *not* an anti-British statement. But like many other people, I feel grossly insulted by people who—in the safety of their established country—turn a rather snobby nose up when someone claims to be fully Irish in a conflicted area such as the North.

Many people have struggled with this issue. The former Formula 1 racing driver Eddie Ervine, who hailed from Ballymena, got into big trouble displaying the Irish tricolour and for being seen as 'Irish' on victory podiums around the world. His family suffered for this display, and Eddie had to compromise. But, correctly in my opinion, we should not expect Irish sporting greats such as Padraig Harrington to be anything other than proud in celebrating their victories as Irishmen, with the tricolour proudly wrapped around their shoulders. Continuing the sporting theme and illustrating the way these things are overtly politicised, we even had some Unionist politicians referring to the 'all British' GAA final between Armagh and Tyrone in 2003. Being Irish in the North can often be difficult.

A similar 'jarring' experience for the Irish in the North is the long-running debate over soccer players from the North declaring they want to play for the Republic of Ireland team. The former Northern Ireland team manager Nigel Worthington spoke of the two teams as being from two different countries. With this totally Unionist approach, Worthington continues the long line of people not seeing the broader picture and acknowledging that Irish people who happened to be born in the North have an inalienable right to play for the Republic. In my political role, I stated this many times in the press when a former Chief Executive of the Irish Football Association (IFA) played the Unionist card and challenged that right. They lost their case, and I got an assurance from the IFA President at a Culture Arts and Leisure Committee meeting in Stormont that any players who decided to opt for the Republic would be respected and not pressurised in any way. It is interesting to note in this context how the young Sunderland star James McLean, from Derry, who opted to play for the Republic of Ireland received sectarian abuse and a 'death threat' on Twitter after expressing his 'pleasure at being selected to play for his country' in the Euro 2012 soccer championships. The failure to see beyond the geography and constitutionality of the North, to the Irish nation and the Irish in the North, is a dreadful failure repeated many times, not just in soccer. I have a feeling that Rory McIlroy will continue to experience some of these tensions such as when a tricolour was recently thrown to him as he finished a golf tournament!

I fully appreciate there have been overlaps and interplays of things Irish and British. How could it be any different with such proximity and political history? I therefore want to turn to the Unionist people, and where they have come from, in the context of partitioned Ireland, and where they stand now.

I have already referred to Irish Unionism becoming Ulster Unionism after partition in 1920 but suffice to say at this point that quite a number of Unionists I have spoken to down through the years have been embarrassed when reminded of this fact. It seems to be a concept that they find hard to come to terms with. On the broader identity question, I have had the opportunity to participate in and witness many personal and professional conversations on this subject, and despite many strong identity statements by Unionists, I believe that if you scratch the surface there is indecisiveness, some would say insecurity, about their true identity. In the dialectic of the various identity-labels; 'Irish', 'British', 'Ulster', 'Northern Irish' and more recently 'Ulster-Scots', I believe there are many question-marks about a people who still need to cling to 'a place apart'. Yet it is that very idea of being 'a place apart' that again, harps back to partition and underscores its inherent divisiveness. British by constitution; Irish by place and being; not totally British by identity; more of an Irish affinity for those regarding themselves as Northern Irish, compared to very little affinity indeed with 'Finchley' – to allude to Margaret Thatcher's rather feeble allegory on the apparent 'true Britishness of the North'.

I have referred to the identity approach of many Unionists who describe themselves as Irish when on holiday but revert to being British when back home. The thought of being grouped in with the infamous 'Brits on tour' was apparently just too much! However for the majority of their lives many Unionists want to hold on to some version of Britishness. One of the more stark examples I heard was in Cairo. I visited the local markets with another person from the North and the traders always asked versions of who we were and where were we from. I obviously responded by confirming I was Irish, whereas the person I was with responded on all occasions with the description "British, but not English". The qualification was illuminating to me, but I am quite sure was totally incomprehensible to the poor spice and vegetable sellers, who certainly didn't get any indication of that person being from the North of Ireland, never mind the island of Ireland. I believe that type of qualification, although not put as explicitly, runs deep in the Unionist psyche: 'being British' has been an inherently-compromised statement by many Unionists in the North.

Even terms such as 'Ulsterman' or 'Ulsterwoman' are qualified. It is not a facetious act to ask a Unionist "Is that six, or-nine-county Ulster?" One might even get a reaction such as that of a senior Ulster Unionist politician in the Belfast Assembly who actually described Northern Ireland as "proper Ulster". This is when identity politics borders on the ridiculous. One gets, as I have had in conversations, one rugby enthusiast glad that Ulster rugby is a nine-county entity, while other enthusiasts give next to no credence to that fact. In addition, it is illuminating to see 'Northern Ireland' flags waved at Ulster rugby matches, far outnumbering genuine Ulster flags and that is even before we take into account the number of Union Jacks also displayed at such matches.

Ulster Unionism, Ulster will fight, Ulster TV, Radio Ulster and all the rest of the attempts to make Northern Ireland and Ulster the same, are compromised terms. The bigger tragedy is that I have met many people, particularly teenagers, both in the early 'troubles' and then in schools in the 1990s, who didn't even realise that Ulster includes Donegal, Monaghan and Cavan.

If we now move to the more recently invoked Ulster-Scots identity, this is where we really see many identity contradictions. I think there should be very specific and professional research within the broader Unionist community on the number of people who are glad to be viewed as Ulster-Scots and support and take part in related cultural practices. I know many that are embarrassed by it. We had the post Good Friday Agreement 'urge to include' and the splashing of money that oiled that process. After years of Unionist derision of Irish language and culture, it was as if there was a headlong rush, by some, to get a language and culture for Unionism. Arguments that there were more Chinese and Polish speakers than Irish speakers suddenly disappeared, when even the dogs on the street knew that very few Unionists spoke the Ulster-Scots 'dialect'; even a Chairperson of the Ulster-Scots Board didn't speak it. Then we had the ultimate negative when an advertisement in Ulster-Scots described the mentally ill as "wee dafties". How excruciatingly embarrassing! And the most important commentary of all was that over the years all the applications for grants by Ulster-Scots organisations and the establishment of an Academy and Board of Ulster-Scots were not organs to boost the broader British identity in the North; rather it was to help promote the much more narrow agenda of Ulster-Scots language, music and culture, and incorporate it into the local, Northern Irish culture.

Of course there is a connection between Ireland, Ulster and Scotland; Dalriada epitomises this. But does it mean there is a particular cohesive Ulster-Scots identity and culture? If you try to argue there is an Ulster-Scots language, how do you handle the existence of the Gaidhlig of Scotland with all the infrastructure of a language and genuine links to the Irish Gaeilge language? Linguists have informed me that Scots Gaidhlig and Irish Gaeilge share a common origin and are approximately 90% similar. So, just how do you address the reality of broader Scots-Irish links or those from Ulster who, even with a strong link to Scotland, still regarded themselves as Irish? The Ulster-Scots community have also tried to claim many people as Ulster-Scots. I remember a collection of banners on a series of Bushmills telegraph poles purporting to promote Ulster-Scots culture: one featured a member of the US Apollo crew that landed on the moon in 1969! I wonder if he knew he was Ulster-Scots American. This type of cultural appropriation does more damage than good to any idea of identity in the Unionist community and the particular links between Ulster people, Scotland and indeed their migration to America.

A broader examination also reveals many tensions and contradictions. The *Social Attitudes in Northern Ireland* series has noted shifts in main identity descriptions within the Protestant-Unionist communities. A fortunate 1968 benchmark study by Edward Moxon Browne showed a more even spread between those Protestants who regarded themselves as Irish, British or Ulster. This hardened as successive studies in 'the Troubles' years demonstrated, with those seeing themselves as Irish falling considerably, and allied to a resultant strengthening of the British label, as well as more people seeing themselves as Northern Irish (I surveyed and brought together this information in my own 1997 doctoral dissertation). This rise in a Northern Irish identity seems to have solidified at in-and-around 18% of the NI population, while the description 'British' has slipped to 39%. Interestingly, this is 3% behind the number within the North who describe themselves as Irish (*Belfast Telegraph* survey 15 March 2010). It will of course be interesting to see future surveys, including analysis of the 2011 Census, for indications of identity labels.

Other more general building blocks of identity and/or social position for Unionists and Loyalists have also been diluted. There are of course still many who regard their Christian denomination as important. However, the fragmented nature of Protestantism, even when church attendance and adherence were strong, was always regarded as a weakness compared with the monolithic Roman Catholic Church; and it is further weakened with the general decline in attendance and religious adherence. The glue of the Orange Order has been weakened to the point of irrelevance in the broader scheme of society. Reduced membership, the disappearing middle and ruling classes and the emblematic Drumcree standoff all demonstrate a different world for the Order's place in the Unionist psyche. There may still be so-called 'high profile' members of the Order, but their tentacles do not spread with the same effect as of old. While there are still many Unionists in the higher echelons of public service and concerns about their power still exist, they will never again be able to totally dominate, in, for example, the police, civil service and local government.

Another important affinity building-block with Britain has been the service of many northerners in the British Army. I of course acknowledge here that many Northern Catholics and indeed people from the South have served in the British Army. I remember as a teenager starting in the world of work, overlapping with the last of the Second World War veterans who were in their last few years of civilian employment: those I knew had served in India and Europe and they were very critical of the way they had been treated by the British state after the war. Despite this, there was a genuine pride in having served in that war, and many northerners will look to the sacrifice of soldiers as a special link. I have no problem respecting that, and I also see the need for a belated recognition of people from Southern counties who served, particularly in the First World War. This was acutely prominent as a result of the Queen's visit to Ireland in May 2011.

But there are two areas where the military service link gets difficult. When one considers that the mainstream British Army, the Ulster Defence Regiment and its successor, the Royal Irish Regiment, were integral to 'the Troubles' in the North, it is no surprise that some automatic polarisation takes place. They are either regarded as brave people, some of whom made the 'supreme sacrifice', or, as being part of the war machine that was responsible for the likes of 'Bloody Sunday', widespread intimidation and the 'dirty war'. These two views cannot be further apart and will remain so for a long time. I know a person who regards himself as a Republican but nevertheless would, as he puts it, 'love to wear a poppy' each year when the dead of the World Wars and other conflicts are commemorated; he would then say that he couldn't because of the very issues I have just described. So the question of identity, in context of pride versus loathing of British Army service, will no doubt be intertwined for many years to come.

However, the second area is a more recent phenomenon and, I think, must be seriously questioned, particularly by those Unionists who put great store in service with the British Army. The Iraq war is largely accepted as being premised on a lie about weapons of mass destruction, and there are serious and justified questions concerning motives behind the war in Afghanistan. Both wars have rendered massive losses and injuries: western media have been strong on recording the thousands of allied army casualties but not so thorough in informing the world about the many more thousands of indigenous victims in those war zones. The nature of going to war has changed. Iraq and Afghanistan are seen as America's agenda backed up by the British, with many looking upon British support in cynical 'poodle' terms. This terminology sits uneasily beside the spectre of parents receiving home their son's or daughter's remains, but I feel there is an important political point here even if it clashes with personal and family trauma.

Why is London sending people to these wars? This question remains virtually unanswered. I have sat in both the Belfast Assembly and in Coleraine Council when Unionist MLAs and councillors have totally brushed aside the politics of war, knowing that it would bring them onto very difficult ground. I had to make a statement in the Belfast Assembly on the death of a Coleraine soldier killed in action in Afghanistan and received criticism for referring to the politics of war, so I have very personal knowledge of this tension. But I still have to say that service to a London-based political agenda is misguided, as it serves Britain's arguably-bloated sense of importance on the world stage. This misguided support from the North also contradicts the ideal of bringing democracy to these beleaguered countries, inasmuch as Britain profits from alliances with some of the most undemocratic and totalitarian regimes in the world in order to bolster a massive arms sales industry, and further other undemocratic aims.

Unionism's subservience to London's agenda is in contradiction of the questioning and individual freedom of thought and speech ethic of Protestantism. This is one area where even I would say that the religious viewpoint is on better ground than the political stance. The following example is not proof positive but it does illustrate this tension of thought. A local young man who knew well that I was as a Republican, confronted me about his Britishness, a large part of which was articulated by his service in the British Army. When I challenged him about the lies which sent him to Iraq, he immediately recoiled, saying he couldn't question "his government". I would never undermine what he thinks is sincere motivation in his life, but I thought how sad it was to hear such a restricted view from a man that could lose his life doing the government's bidding, especially when millions of thinking people now know that the war was a lie.

I think it is time for people who regard themselves as Unionist/Protestant/loyal to Britain to really question secular political masters who send young people to war for such vacuous reasons that prevail in this modern geo-political world. I appreciate this would be a major step for many Unionists in the North, but I also feel it is an essential one.

So, as a conclusion to this short section on identity, and in conjunction with the previous chapters on Unionism's political position, I will now bring together some main points:

- The 1985 Anglo-Irish Agreement and the 1998 Good Friday Agreement prove in serious political terms that the North of Ireland is not 'as British as Finchley'.
- The North has deep political and socio-cultural divisions which are more difficult to eradicate given the respective sizes of the Unionist-Loyalist and Nationalist-Republican communities which in turn are within an extremely small general population, in a similarly-small geographical place.
- The Unionist political project in post-partition Ireland has failed. It has seriously contracted from its earlier domination of the North, to power-sharing with Republicans and Nationalists in a highly-limited and restricted Belfast Assembly and local councils.
- The North is not financially viable, given that it has never paid for itself and is reliant on the block grant from London, which in turn is a system which locks the North into an inability to

successfully generate meaningful income for itself. Taxation goes to London and, even if there are minor methods of producing revenue, the net effect will often be nil given that the block grant could be reduced in parity with the amounts raised. This is not a proper economy in the normal sense.

- The Unionist community has deep identity challenges. Are they British and, if so, what type of Britishness? Are they of Ulster and, if so, is that the province of Ulster or just the six partitioned counties? Are they Irish, or British-and-Irish? Are they Northern Irish, and where does Ulster-Scots sit in this mix?

- While the Protestant label may be important to many in the Unionist community it is not, in the strictly-religious sense of the word, as important to others. Therefore how does that relate to the importance of the Protestant project and the link with Britain and its royalty? There is an increasing secularisation at personal and societal levels in the North, similar to that which has been progressing for decades in Britain itself. So for how much longer can the anachronism of a 'Protestant monarchy' be sustained? Strict Protestant principles underlying the link with Britain are totally out of keeping with a multi-faith and multi-ethnic society. The long-awaited decision to allow spouses of the King or Queen to be Roman Catholic just adds to this conundrum.

- I have seriously questioned the link between the local armed forces and London's agenda. Outside that and the constitutional link, the North's contemporary attachments for those who regard themselves as British are mostly civic in nature. The links to the rest of Ireland are more deeply indigenous, rooted in place, story, experience and social structure. One cannot separate the particular story of six counties of Ireland from the rest of the island, no matter how hard some might try.

- Finally, there is another issue that I haven't touched on yet, that of the changing nature of the Union itself. I will refer to that in more detail in Chapter Eight.

However, it is not always your political opponent that you have to be wary of. Sometimes you need to be equally aware of elements within your own political community, as the next chapter will, I hope, demonstrate.

Chapter Six

The Curse of the Nearest Opponent

The purpose of this book, as stated in the title, is that of promoting the idea of a united Ireland. I have devoted the major part of the preceding two chapters to political and socio-cultural Unionism. But there is also the significant issue as to how the political parties and 'élite' throughout Ireland will promote and argue for that ideal. Many Irish people desiring a united Ireland will perhaps despair at what they perceive as a fundamental lack of effort and focus on the issue by most Irish political parties. But achieving a more focused approach to a united Ireland during the decade of commemorations will be challenged by certain inter-party issues and difficulties, something I will now explore further.

That difficulty is as the chapter title asserts. Rather than trying to win the debate with others, political parties and politicians are usually—some would say permanently—more wary of their nearest opponent. In this particular case, my concern would be that the various Nationalist/Republican parties both North and South of the border are more likely to express difficulties with their nearest political opponent(s) than promote and win the debate with Unionism. I have had many key experiences in party politics, including a front-seat view of 'the nearest-opponent' syndrome, and I would like to bring these to bear to point the way ahead for Irish parties in the hope that political efforts can be combined. Having a seriously diffused Irish party political focus, seriously hampers the goal I am promoting here – something that thousands believe in. 'The curse of the nearest opponent' is not just an

Irish Nationalist/Republican phenomenon; the Unionists have their own version of it between the DUP and Ulster Unionists, and it is a political reality in all jurisdictions that base their politics on the party system. However, pungent differences from the Irish Civil War and 'the Troubles' have resulted in deeply held, and sometime very hostile opinions between parties and individuals, who somewhat ironically, often claim to share the same overall goal of Irish unity. Clearly, we have to find a solution to these political antipathies if parties are to succeed in this commonly-declared goal.

I stress that I am recording the following examples not out of any personal bad feelings. The bigger issue of uniting Ireland is too important to waste time doing that.

I joined the SDLP as the general advances and particular negotiations that ultimately led to the Good Friday Agreement were set in motion. Sean Farren was a fellow constituency member and, as a part of the SDLP's negotiating team, briefed many branch and constituency meetings on political progress during those years. I won election to both the General Council of the party, and later to the Political Management committee. My first public election effort in the 2001 local council elections was successful when I topped the pole in my area of Coleraine Borough Council. The Belfast Assembly was still going through its difficulties and suspensions, so a lot of the political discourse in the early 2000s was carried out at local council level. As one who is very media aware, there were many opportunities for me to become involved in issues that were in effect, outside the remit of the usual councillor diet. I was also employed by the party for a short period in the early 2000s as a Regional Organiser responsible for working in constituencies west of the River Bann, namely Fermanagh, Tyrone, Mid Ulster, Derry City and East Derry, trying to increase the efforts of local branches and constituency personnel. In late 2003 I was the unopposed incoming chairperson of the party.

I list these points to demonstrate that I was very aware of the organisation and direction of the SDLP at the time. I also knew many of the key players from John Hume down and witnessed the various party approaches and attitudes, particularly to Sinn Féin, but also towards the political parties based in the South.

One of the biggest decisions of my life was to leave the SDLP and join Sinn Féin in January 2004. It was after a long period of reflection and a good number of separate conversations with a trusted SDLP member and a similarly trusted SF member. Obviously I knew there would be political and personal fall-out way beyond what could be regarded as the norm for a politician moving from one party to another. But my particular position, that of a former part-time policeman and member of the Orange Order joining Sinn Féin, was a media dream for many reporters, who never failed to describe me with my previous labels. But, as is so often the case, the substance behind the headlines was entirely different. I genuinely felt that the leadership and direction of the SDLP in the latter Hume days and thereafter was poor, and their commitment to a united Ireland had become diluted. In fact, at a party General Council meeting, a prominent SDLP MLA said he didn't "give a damn about a united Ireland". So it is no surprise that another party member described me as 'a more committed united Irelander' than three-quarters of the party. I experienced the tension of considering my options; do I stay and do nothing; stay on as chairperson using the position to influence change; or, do I move to Sinn Féin – that being my only alternative? Many headlines opined about Sinn Féin being anchored to Republican violence, and most of the SDLP people I left behind subscribed to a very negative view of the Sinn Féin party. I am therefore giving the following examples not only to bear out my argument that the SDLP was suffering and declining as a political force, but also to help illustrate 'the curse of the nearest opponent'. I would also stress that subsequent election results and SDLP leadership issues provide the more objective proofs that my analysis at the time was correct.

Many in the SDLP in the late 1990s and early 2000s were worried about the direction of their party. Some drifted off completely without articu-lating why, whilst others remained and became apathetic. As young 'shinners' (members of SF) appeared on TV, SDLP members pressed for new SDLP faces to be involved publicly, and to appear with the likes of the ageing John Hume and Seamus Mallon. SDLP members were not disrespectful to these two giants but everyone knew that fresh blood had to come on board. One lady speaking at a General Council meeting articulated what many members were privately thinking; she claimed that party members hadn't needed to think politically for the previous twenty years, the thinking had been done by the leadership! It is a basic political truism that if leadership transitions are mishandled the organisation and support suffers. When I proposed that other party representatives should be 'profiled', I was asked by John Hume at a General Council meeting, what was profiling?

During these years and throughout peace process negotiations, reports to local and central bodies were extremely critical of Sinn Féin. The general tone was that SF wasn't at the races, they just weren't up to it, and all this was underpinned by a political arrogance that the peace process was basically a SDLP venture. But this was a difficult party position to uphold in light of Sinn Féin's burgeoning electoral advances. Initial SDLP disbelief at the rise of SF was later subsumed by the party becoming crippled by concerns about how to 'handle' rising SF popularity. They were like the proverbial rabbit blinded by the headlights, and losing their own direction in the process.

I was a member of the Political Management Committee and when a report from that committee containing a reference to 'renewed party emphasis on a united Ireland' came before the SDLP General Council, John Hume ran his finger over the key sentence and declared it "dangerous": that was the end of the conversation. I have to admit that it was one of the most disappointing 'political moments' for me. To have genuine concerns brought from a key party strategy committee at that time, and for it to be firmly put to bed by John Hume with one phrase, epitomised for me, the lack of internal debate, analysis and direction.

At local constituency level one member criticised me for referring to both Nationalists *and* Republicans in my press releases; he was worried at any reference to 'republican', as if the party should not think of all constituents within the gambit of those two fluid terms. Many local members spoke viciously about all things Sinn Féin, yet there was no real thinking devoted to setting out the SDLP stall in that area. Elected representatives were many times keener at working with the Unionists and the Alliance party than with Sinn Féin. One SDLP representative even boasted to me of 'singing from the same hymn sheet' as the Ulster Unionists. I totally accept the need for parties to work together often, and I was well able to do it myself. However, when the lack of desire to work with Sinn Féin is based on political enmity, and that in turn pushes you permanently to work with others regardless of political ideology, then clearly, it does considerable damage to the bigger picture.

When I was elected back on to Coleraine Borough Council as a Sinn Féin councillor in 2004, SDLP councillors sometimes refused to support me on basic 'community' issues such as proposals on the provision of sports equipment in a local leisure centre. I would put it as strongly as this: SDLP councillors would at times be 'economic with the truth' so as to avoid supporting some of my proposals. Even allowing for the personal dimension of my situation, I still expected some degree of political maturity from my previous SDLP colleagues for the benefit of the broader community. But even away from political issues it was the same. I remember expressing my condolences to an SDLP councillor on a death within his family circle: he didn't even utter a word of reply and looked right past me. The same person screamed "bastard" at me on a Dublin street when I bid him the time of the day on our way to a National League final between Derry and Kerry in Parnell Park. The good part of that day was a Derry win (apologies to Kerry readers)!

I readily acknowledge that when looking at the much bigger picture John Hume was the definite exception at seeing the need for working with Sinn Féin, but he was often heavily criticised within SDLP circles (and others) for not protecting the party enough during the Hume-Adams meetings. One MLA said to me at the time of the first Assembly that Hume should have "dropped the bastards" (politically) long ago. However, some of the criticisms about John Hume towards the end of his time were justified. That period and the tenure of subsequent party leaders have, I think, proved my point that the party suffered from a fundamental lack of focus and direction. Many respected Mark Durkan for his intelligence but recognised the fact that he was more of an *apparatchik* than a leader. Interestingly, I know of a meeting in the south Belfast home of a senior SDLP member, early in Mark Durkan's leadership, attended by other long-term SDLP MLAs and activists that plotted Durkan's downfall. Margaret Ritchie's subsequent leadership was ineffective and short-lived, leaving Alasdair McDonnell at the helm. It is also interesting in itself that both Durkan and Ritchie, as Irish national-ists, stood down from party leadership of the SDLP to concentrate on their work at Westminster!

A very public demonstration of the overall difficulty between Sinn Féin and the SDLP was provided when former SDLP MLA Declan O'Loan called for a merger between his party and Sinn Féin. He was immediately suspended from his party's Assembly team, but not from the SDLP itself. Two things are relatively important here. Firstly, this was not a call from just O'Loan; members of his North Antrim constituency also put their names to this call, demonstrating that some serious thought was given to the matter before going public. Secondly, this happened in May 2010, many years after ceasefires, the Good Friday Agreement, putting arms beyond use and all the rest of the peace process steps. That clearly indicates that party hostilities still have a long shelf-life. However, those thousands of people wanting a united Ireland are not looking for parties to necessarily merge; they want focus, commitment and co-operation on this most important issue that transcends local rivalries.

Immediately before I left the SDLP I had, by coincidence, separate conversations with two senior party members. One expressed surprise that more of the electorate were asking him what the SDLP's position on a united Ireland was, and that the party would have to get its act together on this issue. The other member said that the party should target Alliance voters by simply getting on with running Northern Ireland. For me, this political schizophrenia summed up their lack of direction at the time.

When I moved to Sinn Féin, I sensed two things at play in terms of their attitudes to the SDLP. Yes, there were longer-term enmities, epitomised by the often used label the 'stoops', shorthand for the 'Stoop Down Low Party'. But the Sinn Féin of 2004 and beyond certainly didn't worry about the SDLP in the same way that the SDLP worried about them. By that time Sinn Féin had scored many political victories and had bigger fish to fry. There were still some pockets of SDLP strength, but the previous SDLP analysis that SF growth was limited to 'greening the west' was seen to be totally naive and inaccurate, as Sinn Féin made gains across the North. So in contrast to the SDLP's concerns about them, Sinn Féin was more relaxed about the SDLP and certainly was setting out its own political stall. This included some pragmatic thinking, for example, the later move by Sinn Féin President Gerry Adams to contest and win the Louth constituency Dáil seat, south of the border. This and other SF successes in the February 2011 Irish general elections rendered 14 Dáil seats, while Fianna Fáil (FF) was decimated along with their former coalition colleagues the Green Party. But I have to say that being relatively relaxed about your nearest opponent is not quite the same as being prepared to really work together for a bigger ideal. Sixteen years in active politics sadly did not provide me with any real evidence that either the SDLP or Sinn Féin was ready to cross that 'Rubicon'. One main difficulty from the SF side is 'the Sinn Féin project'.

Central to the difficulty of achieving maximum co-operation from Sinn Féin at party level is the strength of feeling and commitment towards 'the Sinn Féin project'. I heard this term on many occasions at various elections and concerning other events. That 'project' is to increase political power North and South with the concomitant call to increasing votes, seats and influence. Central leadership figures would have delivered long-winded analysis of this problem, or that electoral possibility, with the central motivation of what has to be done to limit damage or gain ground for 'the Sinn Féin project'. There are those who do think beyond that, to the need to involve others, to work with others, even a dedicated few who describe themselves as Republicans ahead of being Sinn Féiners.

However, the vast majority, and more importantly many of the central leadership of SF, are so dedicated to the party that it is the 'project' that drives them, first and foremost. It is at this point that one looks for the detail of what Sinn Féin intends to do with that anticipated political power and influence. Many within the party say it will help deliver a united Ireland, and I don't doubt their belief, but there are a reasonable number of people that I either worked with or had conversations with, who wonder about the 'next step' for Sinn Féin, beyond increasing seats in Dublin and Belfast. Does Sinn Féin simply intend to administer partition or, is there a master plan to deliver that 'next step' to unity? Once in an election campaign, I had a conversation with a couple of long-standing, behind-the-scenes election workers, who shared some negative views about SF's participation in the Belfast Assembly. At the end of the conversation (which was about the possible 'next steps'), one of the men roughly said: "I'm sure the leadership has it worked out". This dependence and trust in 'the leadership' is strong, but despite Sinn Féin campaigning for a Dáil green paper, hosting numerous conferences and considerable outreach in the US (all of which is laudable in itself), the blueprint from a party so centred on a united Ireland is not actually there. Martin McGuiness has said there should be a vote in the North on the issue anytime between 2016 and 2020/21, that is, during the lifetime of the next Assembly (*Irish Examiner* 30 January 2012). This is all very well, but where is the detailed plan, focus and strategy for the work to attain the goal?

So my main worry is that the Sinn Féin project will ultimately become self-serving, perhaps not intentionally, but over a period of time. This is because 'the SF project' involves getting ahead of the nearest opponent, thereby alienating them, and therefore having a negative effect on the possibility of parties driving together on a serious united Ireland campaign.

And key within their political drive, and something that has a negative effect on the broader front, is again that tension between the 'army' and political mentality in Sinn Féin. One has to admit that the party has made tremendous political gains and many ex-PIRA members have made the transition to be very good representatives. Indeed, there are many more in background positions dedicated to peace and politics. There was of course a strong leadership motivation to bring as many previous combatants with them in the transition, something largely achieved. As a result, I still think that the army mentality prevails and is a main internal driving force that furthers the party 'project'. To this day I do not see the broader thinking in SF that looks beyond that very focused party mentality of simply winning more seats. How will winning more seats help deliver socio-political unity and what are the main points of their arguments to attain that goal? Interestingly, during my time in the Assembly, a very good survey and focus group exercise was carried out by the party among Sinn Féin MLAs and staffers; one of the findings was that the majority of them did not see how their day-to-day Assembly work contributed to the core party goal of unity. Ironically, a working group in the broader party on 'Irish unity' was the least effective of many working groups.

The 'army' effect, of course, has the broader problem of garnering goodwill in Irish communities. As with the evolution of Fianna Fáil and Fine Gael, this will change over time with the younger representatives taking control as 'the Troubles' generation retires, but this will not happen quickly enough for all the debates in the decade of commemorations. Indeed, I foresee tensions between political parties both North and South which no doubt will be played out in public and will be symptomatic of the subject matter of this chapter. Fianna Fáil are already accusing Fine Gael (*Irish Times* 17 Nov 2011) of reducing the commemoration focus on the 1916 Easter Rising, and I believe Sinn Féin will want to generally include, for example, Bobby Sands and other 'troubles' comrades in their narrative of the inspiration derived from 1916 and other important events. The nearest opponents will argue this one out, as already indicated by FF leader, Micheál Martin, who has accused Sinn Féin of "hijacking history and the achievements of the noble people who fought for Ireland in our War of Independence for their own narrow political ends and to justify their terrorist campaign" (*Irish Times* 21 Nov. 2011). Martin also made a hard-hitting speech at his party's 1916 commemoration event at Arbour Hill, Dublin (*Irish Times* 30 April 2012) in which he accused Sinn Féin of prolonging suffering in 'the Troubles' because they delayed embracing democratic politics. No doubt the tensions will continue.

In rounding off these specific comments I want to mention two other things. Firstly, to say that the 'SF project' mentality could become another version of the mistaken 'long-war' mentality, in that the focus of original causes and reasons is somehow lost and, as in the case of the 'long war' mentality, 'the project' becomes self-serving. The Good Friday Agreement was a blueprint to end violence and replace it with just enough political accommodation. Quite clearly it is not a detailed path to unity. That has yet to be worked out. Secondly, I would like to sum up my opinion that while Sinn Féin is obviously an important player, with elected representatives now serving both North and South of the border, its weakness for the broader work of unity rests in the history of its recent past, and in the present negative perceptions of them held by many people in Ireland. This is summed up by a very thoughtful long-term Republican who described Sinn Féin as "nearly a political party". Its evolution will of course continue, but there are large swathes of opinion that want still more evolution before setting aside the negatives of 'revolution', something Paul Cullen successfully reflects when saying the party must "come out of the ghetto" and that its appeal to the middle classes must increase (*Irish Times* 10 Jan. 2012).

Of course another set of nationalist-republican hostilities with a very long shelf-life are the relationships within the political cluster of Fianna Fáil, Fine Gael and Sinn Féin. How could it be any different when one thinks that Gerry Adams' predecessors, in terms of senior historical figures, included all those with the 'DNA' that also became Fine Gael and Fianna Fáil? For example, Sinn Féin President Eamon De Valera described the movement as "the nation organised", which reflected the party's absolute supremacy in the Irish Nationalist-Republican community during 1917-21 and indeed Dev's own symbiotic relationship with the party at that time. But after that amazing time, all changed, with party splits and 'splits of splits' through the incredibly turbulent years which witnessed the Treaty, civil war, Michael Collins' murder and early free-State tensions, all of which led to the three parties having essentially different experiences in the ensuing decades. A convenient but still thorough commentary of this period is provided by Brian Feeney in his book *Sinn Féin: A Hundred Turbulent Years* (O'Brien Press) 2002.

I do not of course have the same personal knowledge of Fianna Fáil and Fine Gael compared with my experiences with the SDLP and Sinn Féin. However, there were always little snippets at hand, and I will refer to these before moving to bigger-picture examples. In the post GFA years, while Bertie Ahern was still FF party leader and Taoiseach, senior SDLP figures identified future Taoiseach Brian Cowan as being strongly against Sinn Féin. They reasoned that they should therefore keep Cowan close to increase SDLP influence in Dublin. Meanwhile, many Fianna Fáil activists helped the SDLP in various elections. I was in conversation with them and saw that their vitriol towards Sinn Féin was deep. But down through the years, between my time living in Dublin and through our Ardrahan connections, there were numerous conversations revealing many examples of the intense differences between Fianna Fáil and Fine Gael. The civil war has obviously rendered some decades-long difficulties.

The crucible period of Irish independence contained all of the following major events and players: Sinn Féin establishing itself as the one-time dominant political party in Ireland; the rise of the Irish Republican Brotherhood (IRB); the subsequent emergence of the IRA; the 1916 Easter Rising; the establishment of the 1st Dáil; the divided opinions on partition, either pro-Treaty or anti-Treaty; the subsequent Irish Civil War; the formation of the new Irish State's army while the IRA still claimed to be the Army of the country; the original refusal of De Valera (as the leader of Sinn Féin) to enter the Dáil, and his subsequent re-emergence with a new Fianna Fáil party whose organisational structure drew from virtually every parish in the country, and which founder member Sean Lemass once described as a 'slightly constitutional party'. Fianna Fáil would become the government party in 1932 declaring former colleagues in the IRA 'illegal' by 1936. So, with that incredible twenty years as the foundation (and more thereafter), one can easily imagine the hostilities, enmities and antagonisms between the main political players and successive generations, especially when one of the key actors, Eamon de Valera, was ever-present through to the 1973 end of his Presidential term, only two years before his death. Whether one is a supporter of De Valera or not, his political reign was extremely influential in the shaping of today's Ireland.

If we now fast-forward to 2010, we get a graphic illustration of how long it has taken for 'civil war' differences between Fianna Fáil and Fine Gael to significantly lessen. The 1922 murder of Michael Collins is commemorated annually at the site of his death at Beal na Blath in West Cork. As a main player in negotiating the Treaty with Great Britain, he is naturally regarded as a forerunner of the Fine Gael party; the commemoration of his death is therefore regarded as a Fine Gael event. However, in 2010, the guest speaker at the event was the late Brian Lenihan, a Fianna Fáil TD and Minister for Finance, who was part of a very strong Fianna Fáil political 'dynasty'. Within a year Brian Lenihan was dead at the tragically early age of 52, losing his battle with cancer and generating an enormous and very understandable outpouring of grief and loss. Interestingly, at the time of his death, it emerged that Brian regarded the invitation to speak at Beal na Blath as the pinnacle of his political career, given the significance of a high-profile Fianna Fáiler being invited to give the main address. He hoped the commemoration could be seen as a further public act of historical reconciliation at one of Irish history's sacred places, and also described the spirit of Collins as the spirit of the nation, which he said, must continue to inspire all in public life, irrespective of party or tradition.

The event itself and these powerful words display both the significance of a ninety years' journey in which the 'curse of the nearest opponent' exerted a heavy weight in Irish politics that required a real paradigm shift in relations, before Lenihan could attend and speak at such a historically poignant event. I have no doubt though, that modern-day differences between these two parties are more-or-less contained within their respective roles as political opponents within the context of southern-Irish politics, and therefore differ considerably from their respective attitudes towards modern-day Sinn Féin.

That difference of course, is 'the Troubles'.

Differences between Fianna Fáil and Fine Gael were ultimately contained in a peaceful South where both parties' main interests manifested themselves, whereas Sinn Féin's modern-day manifestation is utterly embedded in the IRA's role in 'the Troubles' and the violence of that period. Even though the SF party has played a considerable role in the peace process, Fianna Fáil and Fine Gael have more problems with Sinn Féin than they have with each other, especially as Sinn Féin gains more ground in the South. Again, the curse of the nearest opponent looms large.

Violence

If we are to move forward collectively and minimise the curse of the nearest opponent then we have to deal with the extremely important issue of violence. Like so many others, I lived through the violent era and still see political agendas based on views about the violent past being played out nearly two decades after the ceasefires. I know there are many difficult stories, but I also know of the entirely vindictive attitudes on ALL sides, to the deaths of those from 'the other side'. I know of Special Air Service (SAS) members and their RUC special forces colleagues for example, partying for two solid days after they had 'taken out' IRA members; I also know of a Republican sympathiser who phoned Lurgan RUC station asking for a Constable who had been recently killed by the PIRA, and then laughing down the phone; I know Republican supporters who developed a passion for the 'Mull of Kintyre' folk-song after a 1994 helicopter crash killed 25 'intelligence operatives' from the RUC, MI5 and Army on the Mull of Kintyre in Scotland. I similarly know of loyalist celebrations when IRA or Sinn Féin members were killed. Bloody Sunday in Derry was even described as 'good Sunday' by loyalist leader John McKeague at the time. These examples are only those of the hardliners: but there were equally ugly attitudes among the 'great and good' of society, including teachers and doctors, who never publicly sullied their standing, jobs or reputations but nevertheless were delighted when 'the enemy' was killed. War, troubles, conflict, whatever the label, brings out many dreadful attitudes, the accurate and truthful recording of which is unfortunately lost in the noise of the dominant media stories and selective societal memories.

As well as many personal experiences of 'the Troubles', my doctorate thesis examined moral attitudes to state and paramilitary violence from the outbreak of 'the Troubles' in the North, through to the 1994 ceasefires. Through my University employment in international conflict-related projects, I have been fortunate to work with civil society representatives and senior politicians through to President level in Nepal, Basque Country, Serbia and Kosovo. I have also been part of professional networks where I learned about many other conflict areas and the work to resolve many difficult issues. Again, I list these to simply make the point that I hope to bring more than just a local viewpoint to this topic, and indeed to the entire book.

I want to make it very clear that I am not interested in excusing or defending, or making partisan condemnations of violence. Like so many contentious things in life, the debate contained on 'the first page of history' in the media is drastically limited at the time most such incidents happen. For example, and looking beyond Ireland for a moment, I recommend reviewing Fox News, BBC and Al Jezeera coverage of Israel's pounding of Gaza in 2008-9, which will graphically demonstrate how our perceptions can be shaped depending on which storyteller you follow. The first power of media is in that which it excludes, and I feel that exclusions are still made. Accordingly, I feel we need to examine the phenomenon of politically-motivated violence in this context. However, I am not going down the route of a limited partisan debate based on selective memory or on limited media coverage; my agenda is much broader than that. If we are to transcend political differences for the bigger goal of a united Ireland, then this thorny issue simply must be addressed, and in doing so, we must not become negatively consumed by it.

Looking at the bigger picture of politically-motivated violence there are three main parts to a period of conflict. Firstly, there are the circumstances that lead to the slide into violence and the initial brutality. Secondly, a mutually-reinforcing cycle of violence unfolds, in which the original issues are lost and competing sides battle for supremacy. Thirdly comes, the work that leads to cessation of the armed campaign, and hopefully a transition to peace. Quite clearly not all fall neatly into a theory like this on a page, but by-and-large this three-stage paradigm helps us. The middle period is perhaps the darkest of the dark because society is shattered, going nowhere, caught in that meaningless cycle of violence as the conflict settles into a macabre power-struggle between sides that are in it for the long haul, where 'losing' is not an option! I would identify the mid/late seventies and throughout most of the eighties as being the second period in Northern Ireland. The third part is when political 'back–channels' are used to build communication between the competing sides: this period can be very frustrating for the public, as they largely only see the same old cycle of victims and casualties, while all those in authority can do is give limited and hopeful messages in an environment which appears to have little or no hope. Gradually that changes however, and more hope can be garnered. The late eighties into the nineties are the years in the North that equate with this third period.

But we need to concentrate more on the first part, the slide into violence and its initial brutality, because all that followed flowed from there. I stress again this is not to excuse or defend anything; I think the slide into violence in Northern Ireland was an undeniable and brutal reality. But a wider point pertains here because there is always a debate about the physical-force tradition in Ireland, a debate that generally goes round in circles. For example, was Michael Collins' violence more justifiable in the 1920s than Martin McGuiness's subsequent IRA activities? This is the type of question that epitomises the insoluble conundrum that repeatedly sours nationalist/republican party relations. I am not saying that I can categorically resolve these questions in this book, but I think there are some features worthy of consideration here.

I employed two phrases earlier in the book. These were, 'being Irish in the North', used purposely to take the emphasis away from a religious label, while simultaneously stressing that it was largely Irish people who suffered discrimination. Secondly, I used the phrase 'partitioning of experiences' to emphasise the very different experiences between Irish people in the North and of those in the South, in the decades following partition. In employing these phrases I first had to ask if Irish people in Kilkenny for example, had been refused jobs by biased employers because they were Irish; or if Irish people in Dublin had been allocated the worst housing; or if Irish people in Mayo had suffered a warped election system; or if Irish people in Wexford had been treated as second class citizens; or if Irish people in Kerry had been beaten off the streets as they marched for civil rights; or if Irish people in Tipperary were stoned by people who would never be charged for their criminal actions; or if Irish people from Galway had been shot for marching against internment, and so the rhetorical questions could continue!

Before taking this approach further let me make two things very clear. Firstly, I am not stating that everything was simplistically one-sided, but the historical facts of the situation should not be denied or glossed-over. On the Nationalist/Republican side there was of course tension between those who were campaigning peacefully, and those who would exploit the melting-pot atmosphere. For example, the Provisional IRA has since admitted that the conditions for a sustained armed struggle failed to materialise until the attempted repression of the Civil Rights movement (IRA Code of Conduct 1987 recorded in Martin Dillon, *The Enemy Within*, Doubleday 1994, 279). Secondly, I am not trying to present some vague proposition by rhetoric. We need to ask ourselves the fundamental question; what would the reaction have been, if in 1969, over 80% of the people displaced and the damage caused had been inflicted on Irish people in the abovementioned (southern) Irish towns and cities? (Figures are recorded in Jonathan Bardon's recording of facts of Catholic families and properties affected, in *A History of Ulster* Blackstaff Press 1992, 671). Would those communities have risen up against such treatment? Could a slide into deeper violence then have occurred? I believe it could, and this point is not just about semantics or rhetoric.

The point is very firmly embedded in the biggest difference of all: in the experiences of Irish people on either side of the partition border. Being Irish in the North was, for most, about being definitively second class; being Irish in the South was an entirely different experience.

As 1969 rolled into 1970, the IRA came to the fore, and there is no doubt that their actions were seen then in a much more benign way, compared with the later 1970s and onwards. Two examples graphically illustrate this point. Father O'Donnell, a priest in the Ardoyne area of North Belfast, said that the only hope of protection was in the IRA, as both Stormont and Westminster appeared to advocate a policy of violence towards the Nationalist community (Irish Times, 22 Nov 1971). A decade later, and having had time to reflect on the slide into sectarian violence, Cardinal Cathal Daly commented that those who mobilised the Provisionals in 1970 "must now have difficulty in recognising it as the same movement" (*Irish Times* 1 & 2 Jan 1980). So the overall question is this. Had the pre 1969/70 conditions that existed for Irish people in the North also pertained to Irish people in the South, could the results have been similar? I think they could.

I appreciate that readers and commentators may argue that much has happened since then and we cannot live in the past, harking back to 1969/70. I generally agree, but when it comes to the legacy of Irish, British and Unionist violence down through the different eras I am asking two things. Firstly, let us not see 'the Troubles' as some distant tribal-sectarian war that was separate from the rest of us and happened 'up there', because that isolates the dreadful experiences of Irish people who just happened to be born into the North. Secondly, let us not reduce our analysis of violence to the headline events that are brought to our attention, because as we have seen, different competing groups will use different headlines for very different agendas.

I think these tensions of thought were graphically epitomised in the 2011 presidential campaign in the South when Fine Gael candidate Gay Mitchell decided as a campaign tactic, that he should regularly challenge Sinn Féin candidate Martin McGuiness. In one interview he basically blamed McGuiness and the IRA for 'the Troubles'. His political agenda couldn't countenance proposing other contributing reasons such as partition, Unionist misrule, the manifest aggression of militant Unionism, and the institutional injustices of Unionist/British rule. Martina Devlin gave an extremely insightful view on this (*Irish Independent* 6 Oct 2011). She wrote that the debate about the North, which hadn't properly taken place at the time of the Good Friday Agreement, was now becoming intertwined with the presidential race in the Republic. In my view Martina was correct, and so the 'curse of the nearest opponent' completely dominated the issue, rather than the public receiving a balanced view!

As this is such an emotive issue I want to add two points. Firstly, the presidential campaign of Martin McGuiness was being constantly benchmarked—by his opponents and the media—against his IRA past. The result of the election showed that while McGuiness claimed it was a great campaign for his party, he did not make the expected inroads and attract much more than core SF support in the South. His past connections along with high profile interventions such as that by David Kelly (the son of Irish Army soldier Private Patrick Kelly killed by the IRA in 1983), again graphically demonstrated longstanding attitudes of antipathy and negativity towards Republican violence, among voters in the South.

Secondly, I think that the evolution of the PIRA as a 'defender' of the Nationalist community to becoming a ruthless killing machine is a very significant point. My personal opinion is that the PIRA, in the mid to late seventies, badly miscalculated socio-political reactions in the South; in the eyes of most southern communities, the PIRA's 'Irish' struggle had become a very Northern struggle. An anecdotal reminder of this perception was a lady in conversation with me describing 'the Troubles' as "the Belfast war".

But I also think that the PIRA was out-foxed by the British. When the policy of Ulsterisation was introduced in 1978, bringing the RUC and other local security force sectors to the forefront of the 'fight against terrorism', the paradigm shift was not matched by Republican thinking. Obviously there were many RUC victims before this and many British soldier casualties after it. However, for an organisation that claims to understand the historical motivation and effects of 'leaving us our patriot dead' Republicans left many 'unionist patriot dead' in graveyards around the North. They also made other fundamental mistakes. By viewing the Protestant-Unionist community as 'the British presence in Ireland'; by adopting the 'long war' attitude and associated campaign; and by confusing their localised struggle for an 'Irish struggle', Republicans caused and fuelled, deeply-embedded and negative attitudes, particularly among the Unionist community and many in the South of Ireland.

However, if Irish political parties, Irish commentators and Irish communities can all 'move on' in terms of their relationships with Unionists and the British, surely it is time for similar approaches to evolve amongst all those who now want to peacefully work for a united Ireland? Parties are neither being asked to totally agree with each other, nor to forget the victims of 'the Troubles' and the ever-important quest for truth, but this work for a united Ireland totally and utterly transcends one political party, one group, one community or any one partisan agenda. If we don't somehow overcome 'the curse of the nearest opponent' it will remain a long-term barrier, and may even become the long-term winner.

Integral to that sense of moving on is the reclamation of the word 'republican'. I remember my wife describing herself as a republican to a lady she knew reasonably well. The conversation took place after the Good Friday Agreement, but the lady was still quite shocked at this definition; it was very obvious that she immediately equated the term republican with violence. When she expressed displeasure, Valerie immediately asked her; "Don't you want to live in a united Ireland which elects its own President?" She agreed of course, and accepted that in that context she was, in effect, a republican at heart, or at least an aspiring one! I acknowledge there are many more issues to discuss in the needed debate on republicanism. However, that particular casual conversation epitomises the difficulty and need for republicanism to re-evaluate its place and image in Irish society, and not be the sole preserve of just one political party or movement that desires a united Ireland.

But the reclamation of the term 'republicanism' not only relates to the question of violence; it also relates to all the 'Celtic Tiger' negatives that have damaged the image of the Irish Republic locally and internationally, particularly the unbridled individualism of that era and the cosy, self-serving relationships between certain politicians, bankers and developers. This in turn led to the recession and highlights the need for an urgent and necessary conversation in Irish society about its new place on the global stage. Many in Ireland want to re-focus for the future and examine what we want for a genuine republic. There is a belief that we need a renewal of the republican ideal, including reclaiming all that was good in different eras, even going back to some central principles from the 1798 vision of republicanism.

All of these issues will, I believe, present many opportunities in the years ahead so I will concentrate on them in the next two chapters.

Chapter Seven

A United Ireland

What might the governance of a united Ireland look like? This is a big question with all of the main aspects being massive issues in themselves. In approaching some of them, I hope to distil the main issues that always come to the fore. In general, these concern the constitution, governance and finance, the latter of which will be dealt with in more detail in Chapter Eight. I appreciate there are many and varied opinions on these issues; I am articulating mine in the spirit of making a contribution as I outlined in the Introduction. But I do feel that I have to point out that too many people or organisations espousing Irish unity have not put 'meat on the bones' so-to-speak; I feel it is essential that we do, and that is what this chapter is about.

Constitutional Position and Government Structures

The present Irish Constitution contains much that is good, progressive and democratic. However, many in the North negatively associate the Irish Constitution with two things. Firstly, the previous reference in the Constitution to the 'special place of the Catholic Church' in the South, an issue long dealt with by the Fifth Amendment of the Irish Constitution in 1972 which removed that reference. Secondly, the controversial debate over the former Articles 2 and 3 of the Constitution which in essence defined the Irish nation in terms of the territory of the entire island, a position Unionists viewed as an aggressive claim. These were amended, as a result of the 1998 Good Friday Agreement, with two central implications. The right to be part of the Irish nation is granted to all those born on the island of Ireland thus changing the emphasis of the nation from a territorial statement to a people-centred one. Secondly the amendment then outlined the desire for Irish unification by peaceful means and "with the consent of a majority of the people, democratically expressed, in both jurisdictions in the island."

In the context of future change a written constitution, while as natural as air to people in the Republic, would I think, be a statement of its time for all in a united Ireland and thus be of help to those presently regarding themselves as Unionist and/or Protestant.

I also want to put the possibility of change into a larger context. The understandable 'societal depression' that descended on people in the South as a result of the recession, linking national budgets and IMF issues, has brought much discussion about, for example, what President Michael D Higgins has called a 'real republic', a theme strongly articulated at his inauguration on 11 November 2011. Others have put it in terms of a 'second republic'. Many of the ideas for change preceded the recession, but there is absolutely no doubt that the excesses of the 'Celtic Tiger' era led to an understandable public distrust of politicians and bankers and the systems they represent. This in turn has given a renewed impetus to a desire for radical change. For example, the Dublin City Business Association published a collection of papers entitled *A Ten Point Manifesto: Towards a Second Republic* in February 2011. In addition, Peadar Kirby and Mary Murphy published their book *Towards a Second Republic: Irish Politics after the Celtic Tiger* (Pluto Press, 2011), and this I feel has made a particular and excellent contribution on the subject of reform. Both works referred to numerous other contributors to this debate, and I acknowledge those sources for some of the ideas contained in what follows.

I am of course including N Ireland in my thoughts on the 'second republic' and, to their credit, Kirby and Murphy did likewise. Despite arriving at a different conclusion to mine, arguing, basically, that there is little likelihood of a second Irish Republic overcoming the past divisions of Northern Ireland in the foreseeable future (pp. 226-8), I will nevertheless press ahead optimistically with the following thoughts. I know the

Irish Government's planned Constitution Convention will result in changes and that other suggestions may come to light in any negotiation phase prior to Irish unity, but I feel that whatever changes are made, equality must be at the heart of our Constitution. I would also propose the following two points.

The first is embedding meaningful Freedom of Information (FOI) provisions into the present Constitution. I have used the Freedom of Information process in the North and I have to say I was bitterly disappointed, both in the bodies deemed 'legally' outside its remit, and the lack of real teeth if one is to appeal against an organisation that is officially 'subject to FOI' but then claims a particular exemption from the legislation. Governments have always had an interest in protecting those they need to protect, while hypocritically lauding legislation as progressive. I know of many similarly-frustrated people in the South who have understandable complaints about FOI provisions: this is no surprise. British-influenced legislation in the North and a secretive Dublin administration, which is merely an afterglow of the British secretive approach to government, leaves a severely restricted Irish FOI system. Transparency, or the lack of it, is ultimately controlled by a very centrist and secretive administration. When a senior civil servant writes under a *nom de plume* about the culture of secrecy in Irish politics still being alive and well in 2011 (*Irish Times* 4 Oct 2011), it is very clear we need meaningful change.

The Swedish FOI provisions are often cited as an excellent model. The two works I referred to previously either speak of the need for a better FOI system in Ireland or, express support for Stockholm's model and give examples of how it could help transparency here. I think that sensibly implementing best practices from this model and other worthy systems would be of benefit to all. Ireland's people are at a point where they are disgusted at how vital information about many issues, in particular the banks that virtually broke the country, could only come out by tragic drip-feed and step-by-embarrassing-step, until the IMF literally stepped up to the door. Surely society cannot accept that again. I am not claiming that embedding meaningful Freedom of Information provisions in the Constitution is the panacea, but I am claiming it is a very important step that is wholly relevant to all present citizens, and hopefully, to all future Irish citizens.

The second core constitutional provision I would propose is that of upholding cultural rights. Quite clearly this has important resonances, but is not exclusively for, those regarding themselves as Protestant/Ulster/British coming into a united Ireland. Many might regard this area as difficult and international experience has admittedly displayed some tensions in this regard, but again, I feel that if handled professionally and genuinely it can be a positive step. Cultural rights do not contradict the important and standard human rights contained in domestic legislation or in international measures to which Ireland subscribes. They should also be distinguished from fundamental rights to non-discrimination and from affirmative action policies, as classically proposed by experts in the field. Emphasising cultural rights in the Constitution is neither a sop to, nor something artificial for the Protestant community; rather it is about making a national, corporate statement which accepts the importance and articulation of different cultural practices. In this manner, including a 'cultural rights' clause in the Constitution offers a unique opportunity to identify and describe cultural attachments; it will also endorse 'diversity' as a constitutional principle, and enshrine and safeguard those attachments for Protestants in particular, by including an accommodation for minorities in the highest possible statement by our nation.

Central Structures

I would propose that a united Ireland should have a central Dáil/Parliament in Dublin. This automatically sets out my stall against a 'federal solution' which proposes a layer of government in the four Irish provinces of Ulster, Munster, Leinster and Connaught. My objections to this federal model are based on numerous, valid complaints about excessive government and administration over the years, and not surprisingly this controversy heightened during the dreadful downturn. Readers in Ireland will immediately identify with ongoing arguments about too many Teachtaí Dála (TDs), MPs, MLAs and councillors, and related issues such as double-jobbing, expense scandals and bloated semi-state bodies, inefficient public agencies, quangos and the civil service. I therefore think that the public at large would not be enamoured by the multiple layers of government at the following levels: local councils, four provincial administrations, Dublin government, an upper House (a point to which I will return) and European Parliament representatives. All of these of course come with their related expenses, offices, staff and expensive machinery. One can imagine trying to sell the idea of unity to the media and everyone in the State – regardless of the labels 'Republican', 'Unionist', 'southerner', 'northerner' or whatever—and being told to pay for this excessive representation. I just think it would be a totally unacceptable idea all-round, and rightly so.

My position also sets out my stall against a Belfast Assembly in a united Ireland. Some have said that northern Unionists need to have the Belfast Assembly, that if there is devolution from London to Belfast in a UK situation there should be corresponding devolution from Dublin to Belfast in a united Ireland scenario. However, I feel that in more recent years the debate has moved on considerably. With growing positive engagement between politicians, even on the limited North-South bodies, and with safeguards in an agreed written constitution and other mechanisms, people in the North can be satisfied with a Dublin government and administration balanced with sound local government machinery. I do not think that a vote for unity would be lost on the Belfast Assembly issue if put genuinely to the people.

But I do strongly feel that there is need for reform of the Dáil, something that would appeal to virtually everyone, such is the feeling in Ireland in this era. Much commentary was understandably made on how well-paid representatives in the national government in Dublin were actively dealing with the proverbial local pot-holes to protect local votes while banks were not sufficiently regulated, acting like casinos.

With all due respect to the Kennedy clan in the US, local politics is of course important, but all politics is not local, as the bursting of the Celtic Tiger bubble has graphically shown. How could Government policy be so skewed to the massive and destructive own goal of wild, unsustainable property development in the face of local and international warnings about the economic imbalance? Kirby and Murphy reflected the negative effect of the Irish system with their description of it as a 'centralised state with a localised electoral system' (p24). It is vital we not only get the balance right between the important layers of Government but also equip all levels with appropriate laws and regulations. Members of the Dáil cannot be embroiled in local 'pot-hole' politics to the point of neglecting bigger-picture national questions. Neither can they be deemed to be expert in all fields: it follows that professional expertise can be lacking in decision making on vital national and international questions.

Therefore we must blend how we structure our Dáil to include professionalism but also retain public accountability.

Again referring to the key works on a 'second republic', I contend that Ireland has a dual problem of too many TDs and a conspicuous lack of trust in politicians and the prevailing political ethos. I feel we have the opportunity to be both critically introspective and radical, and thereby positively reform for our future. I would therefore add my voice to some ideas already articulated by others and personally propose additions or nuances as follows.

Ireland should have fewer TDs, and their roles should concentrate on national, international matters and linking legislation. There are many references to other European countries and their ratio of political representatives to population, and there is little doubt that we could move 'up the league table' in this regard. I acknowledge that if Irish unity were to come about this would again increase numbers, but the agreed TD ratio to population formula could be maintained in that scenario.

Two additional measures could introduce more expertise to Dáil/Government deliberations and actions. Firstly, as others have proposed, the number of full ministerial cabinet posts could be reduced and the number of ministers of state could be increased. The latter measure could more easily lead to a greater number of non-elected people with appropriate experience being appointed as ministers of state and thereby bringing that experience, motivation and vision to the work of Government. There will of course be debate about number permutations, but I feel that we should accept the principle and work our way through the debate to a full solution.

The second idea would be to introduce non-elected members to the Dáil committee system. These key committees should be revised to ensure they really do hold a minister and his/her department to account, but I would also be of the opinion that two non-elected professional people on each committee could deliver much added value. Let me give an example. One of the saddest indictments of politicians was the lack of financial knowledge and foresight. If two professionals had been on the appropriate Dáil Finance Committee, could the questioning and challenges been better directed? Could more issues have been raised in the Committee? Could they have queried the stark imbalance of the unsustainable tax-take from the development boom, and would their contribution have been less protective of the political status-quo?

As I have already pointed out, I served on the Departmental Committee system in the Belfast Assembly. I believe it is a relatively good system, but there is undoubtedly a difference when the Minister from your own party comes before the Committee. Independent professionals could therefore bring a greater freedom to question the Ministers and officials. As always we would have the practical problem of selecting people from a relatively small 'civic gene pool', but surely we can set up a system that both delivers and avoids the 'golden circle' problem.

The question of an upper house looms. There was a senate in the old Unionist regime in the North, and of course a senate is part of the South's current political machinery, although there is a lot of debate about its abolition: current Taoiseach Enda Kenny has promised a referendum on the issue. I personally think that the Senate as currently established could be replaced to meet the new paradigm of a second republic / united Ireland, and I feel that the replacement 'vehicle' could positively help deal with not only northern Protestant fears but also those of the citizens generally.

One of the key responsibilities, or perhaps sole responsibility, of this new body should be examining and adjudicating on petitions by citizens on matters of concern. I am largely basing this idea on the European Parliament's Petitions Committee, although most definitely not recommending we simply duplicate it. However, it is impressive that an EU citizen can go directly to this body, which will, if appropriate, investigate a complaint that some action by a member state contravenes EU law. I had one experience of lodging such a petition on an important local issue. I was impressed that my initial access to the system was straightforward; I could personally present my case to the Parliament's Petition Committee in Brussels and challenge the appropriate department in Belfast by my petition, all of which contrasts with our general view of EU machinery as a giant bureaucracy distant from the ordinary individual.

Similarly, I feel that if a body in Ireland received, investigated and adjudicated on concerns raised by citizens, accountability would increase and therefore it would be both more meaningful to the people and a positive contrast to the present Senate. I also believe it would have a balancing effect between citizens' rights and the role of the Dáil, something that was highlighted by concerns in the Referendum 2011 question on inquiries by the Oireachtas, which was defeated. That defeat has thrown the transition of the Oireachtas Committees on Investigations, Oversight and Petitions to the Oversight Committee with extended powers into a stasis. I appreciate that the term Oireachtas in that context included both the Dáil and Senate but I am writing in the context of a replaced Senate. The mechanism I am proposing is, I believe, a worthwhile suggestion to be considered as it goes to the heart of accountability for citizens.

Naturally there are practicalities to this idea, for example, ensuring there is no clash with the Ombudsman's role, which is restricted firstly by the list of issues it cannot investigate and secondly by only being permitted to recommend actions.

For convenience I will call this proposed body the 'Petitions Board', so what could the broad principles of its remit be? I feel that individuals could lodge a petition if they felt their constitutional safeguards were being violated. This would immediately ensure that it was not inundated with smaller queries and challenges to departments that can be made by other means, therefore making a substantial contribution to civic life in Ireland, rather than being more of the same. There would be guidelines on how petitions are lodged and investigated, the manner in which people exercise their right to appear before the body, or a representative part of, and how adjudications are made and their legal standing should individuals want to further pursue the matters in the domestic or international courts.

Quite clearly the devil in is the detail, but mentioning two scenarios could help take this a little further than raw theory. Given that the main thrust of the book is about uniting Ireland and that would mean those people currently regarding themselves as Protestant/Unionist/British becoming part of the new nation, I would like to give this one illustration which is relevant to them.

If there were an article in the Constitution on cultural rights as I proposed, then a person from that group could raise a petition outlining her/his reasons as to why the appropriate constitutional provision is being violated by act of commission or omission by an arm of the government. That person would have the right to appear before the 'Petitions Board' and outline his/her case. The Board would have a duty to investigate the regulations, legislation and the actions or inactions of those cited in the petition and adjudicate on the issue. This avenue would of course be opened to all ethnic groups.

Furthermore, one could envisage any citizen petitioning on the role of organisations on aspects of social justice. Article 45(1) of the present Constitution says "the State shall strive to promote the welfare of the whole people by securing and protecting as effectively as it may a social order in which justice and charity shall inform all the institutions of the national life". It is unfortunate, even tragic, that most of the aspirations which underpin these words were jettisoned during the Celtic Tiger. I think the achievement of a united Ireland, or earlier, would be a time to re-focus on such ideals. In this context, part of that process could be a petition on, for example, the role and effect of the Financial Regulator or the various bodies that are meant to safeguard societal welfare or a part thereof.

Social justice provisions in Section 45 of the Constitution also refer to the following areas: providing adequate livelihoods, control of material resources, free competition not leading to mass ownership by the few, credit control aimed at the welfare of the people (if only!), and private enterprise directed not to be exploitative. These all highlight areas of concern on which petitions could be raised and demonstrate possibilities for protecting citizens and giving this body much more day-to-day relevance than the present Senate. However, there are three other relevant points to be made, as follows.

The first is the relationship between the 'Petitions Board' and the Supreme Court as the court with jurisdiction to ensure constitutional compliance by governmental bodies and private citizens. It must be recognised that, while obviously of very important legal consequence, the Supreme Court has a limited remit. It hears appeals from the High Court, the Court of Criminal Appeal and the Courts-Martial Appeal Court, the last two being severely restricted. The Supreme Court also hears points of law referred to it from the Circuit Court. I therefore envisage the role of a 'Petitions Board' as follows: far from clashing with the Supreme Court, it would address more of the citizens' day-to-day concerns about how they are being failed in the implementation of the

Constitution's provisions. I could also see over a period of time the 'Board' building up a citizen-centred approach and benchmarks on the Constitution's imminent effect on the people. Naturally, if a petitioner's case was taken further along the legal route then the 'Board's' expressed opinion could be taken into account.

Secondly, there is the standing of Board adjudications. This is a very difficult issue as our society doesn't need another ineffective body expressing opinions which are ignored and merely collect dust: there is absolutely no sense in increasing peoples' frustrations with and cynicism about meaningless measures. Government needs to react positively to its adjudications: these could be to stop or carry out recommended actions. I fully realise there would much debate on a new approach such as this, but I would propose the following central principle.

The Board's adjudications should, where possible, carry a legal and/or procedural weight directing departments to act and, if they don't, the petitioner would have a right of appeal to an appropriate level of court or tribunal. I fully appreciate that if this idea or derivative of it were to ever gain 'traction' there would be strong voices arguing for and against maximum powers of adjudication; these natural reactions would simply have to be debated and a conclusion reached.

Lastly, the make-up of such a group should be partially elected and partially appointed. Concerns about the anachronistic election system to the Senate would be dealt with by direct elections of the people, perhaps at the time of a general election so that both can be carried out on the same day for the same term. The appointed members should be a balanced blend of legal and public service people with experience to reflect the potential work of the 'Board'.

Local Structures

The thrust of my analysis of central structures included more profession-alism, more accountability and the directing of efforts to the 'bigger issues': it follows that local government is the arena for dealing with local problems and day-to-day constituency efforts. I am not totally divorcing TDs from constituencies and constituents, but never again can we go back to the scenario of national representatives being so busy or obsessed with 'votes via pot-holes'. I do not say this to demean the work

112

at local level of local representatives; I place their efforts high on the scale of public service and commitment. I have done that job and know of the sacrifices made by busy local councillors, especially when they are also working in separate full-time jobs to pay the bills.

However, achieving an effective local council network is a massive challenge. Numbers of councils, councillors and staff and the resources available are hot topics. People do get exercised if their 'more local forum' is under threat. In 1992/3 I proposed to what became the Opsahl Report (*A Citizens' Inquiry: The Opsahl Report On Northern* Ireland, ed., Andy Pollak, Lilliput Press, Dublin, 1993) that there should only be seven councils in the North, one for each county and the seventh for Belfast City. When it came, years later, to the very costly process of examining possible permutations for local government in the North to run from 2011 onwards, a seven-council permutation was rejected and an eleven-council proposal failed, amidst great debate about localism (this may be coming back on to the agenda). So one can see that it is much harder to consider and propose change at local level than deliver it. I am therefore not entering the very detailed debate of county council and town councils, but I would say the overall goal should be a lean, effective and accountable system that avoids needless duplication and waste of resources.

I would therefore start my thinking on local government in a united Ireland as being county council driven with perhaps the exceptions being the main cities. They could then actively and meaningfully co-operate (not create another bureaucratic layer) on a provincial basis to bring economies of scale to such issues as procurement, staff for common services, promotion of tourism and local business development. I worked in the 26-council system in the North, and I have to say that when one considered 26 chief executives, corresponding numbers of senior management, tourism and economic development plans (and other issues) for such restricted areas, it was ridiculous. For example, the North Coast with obvious tourism potential was administratively divided into three council areas, numerous local tourism organisations, the NI Tourist Board and ultimately Tourism Ireland, and that was before we got to Donegal: such nonsense should be avoided.

Another key issue that I would advocate is giving councils the maximum legal standing and powers to deliver as many local services as possible.

People will therefore bring the majority of day-to-day enquiries on planning, housing, roads and municipal services to that forum. Powers should be underpinned by requirements for councils to act for all their citizens equally. This is obviously more of a hang-up from the North, where councils acted poorly and equality legislation was one of those measures that helped move things forward with varying degrees of positivity. Councils should effectively engage with the community and voluntary sector, something which I believe is essential but can also be done without creating costly 'systems'.

Kirby and Murphy (pp. 56-7) rightly identified local government reform as a major requirement in a 'second republic', given the lack of local revenue raising powers and key functions such as health, education and policing still being held centrally. They were also rightly concerned about the power of county and city managers, effectively the chief executives of the councils. This clash of executive power with democratic accountability is graphically epitomised by the Dublin City Manager ignoring the vote of Dublin Council and privatising bin collection services in Dublin from January 2012. Whatever one's opinions are on the issues, including the underpinning legislation, the principle and practice in this example is, to say the least, worrying to democrats. Describing present local government structures as the "pawn of central government", Kirby and Murphy very adequately sum up the need for and extent of change that is required to move things forward in a meaningful way for both local communities and in the bigger picture of improved governance across the island .

General

Overall these approaches could combat the much maligned 'parish-pump politics' and increase professionalism and accountability. Central politics would be national and international; local politics would be driven by service delivery and equality, and the 'Petitions Board' idea would be accountability driven. Again, I would stress there are other serious issues to be debated, as they too could contribute to reform. For example, a question that has to be answered is: Does the single transferable vote (STV) system itself propagate the 'parish-pump' approach, in that TDs have to look over their shoulders at party colleagues in the same constituency, never mind TDs of other parties? Perhaps alternatives have to be genuinely considered, but this is part of a debate that will continue regardless of my work here.

Returning then to the northern Protestants in particular, I would stress that the above suggestions would deliver the following for them. Those elected to the Dublin government from northern constituencies would exercise real powers when compared to the limited role they have in the Belfast Assembly, a limitation not compensated for by the small numbers and effect of MPs at Westminster. They would work on the total gambit of national, EU, international and finance matters as equals, and thus not be restricted to a glorified county council dependent upon the real political and economic power brokers in London. They would be working more effectively than ever before on EU matters, especially agriculture and fisheries, therefore no longer being the coat-tail of London and sometimes even the ignored coat-tail.

Secondly, their feeling of localism could be protected in meaningful equality-based local councils wielding more power than presently; the 'bins and burial' role of local councils in the North could be consigned to history. Furthermore, I can foresee over time that blend of localism and national power enhancing the feeling of the Protestants' sense of place and history in Ireland as a whole. The inclusion of non-elected people as ministers of state, in Dáil Committees and on the Petitions Board would also give possibilities for some others to be involved in important and constructive roles. The presence of the 'Petitions Board' itself would also give another source of protection of their cultural rights.

However, I must also stress that the above suggestions are not just about possibilities for northern Protestants deciding for a united Ireland. I have proposed them in the belief that with the appropriate detail added to the core thoughts they would render benefits for everyone in Ireland.

I will end this chapter by briefly referring to religion. It is a relief to say 'briefly' as I think religious tensions of past eras have greatly eased and we live in different times from those when church controls, influences and fears of each other were dominant influences when debating virtually all Irish issues. In the North church attendance is down, Protestant churches' influence is not as strong as it once was and, despite having within the Christian family a strong evangelical sector which makes the news more for the bizarre (such as Rihanna making a video in a field near Bangor), it is clear that religion's social power has waned.

Even Sunday has for a long time moved on from being a shut-down and lock-up day. While personal faith is still very important to many, religious influence is largely kept to the personal realm. Relations between the Protestant churches and the Roman Catholic Church have largely improved. I am not saying that sectarianism has been obliterated, sadly that is not the case, but its ugly influence is localised and minimal rather than the bad old days of it being institutionalised.

The picture in the South has also changed. Attendance at Mass is likewise down. For example, it is estimated that only one in seven of the Dublin Catholic population attend weekend mass (*Irish Times* 14 Dec. 2011). When Archbishop Diarmuid Martin of Dublin reflects that perhaps the Roman Catholic Church in Ireland is already a minority church (*Irish Times* 11 May 2012) it is clear that significant change has occurred before our eyes. In addition the clerical sex abuse scandals and disgust at the way the Irish and Vatican hierarchies dealt with them have utterly reduced the influence the Roman Catholic Church had in this society. The latest controversy, (*BBC – This World* documentary 1 May 2012 & *Irish Times* 8 May 2012) on how Cardinal Seán Brady (then as Father Brady) handled or mishandled complaints of sexual abuse by the infamous Fr. Brendan Smyth in 1975, continues to demonstrate the extremely negative impact on public opinion towards the Church. It is ironic that an establishment that attempted to, and many would say did, control sexual behaviour could be 'brought to its knees' by the sexual behaviour of some of its own priests. This is totally epitomised by the very belated revelation (*Irish Times*, 8 Dec. 2011) that allegations of child sexual abuse were made against the late Catholic Archbishop of Dublin, John Charles McQuaid, one of the most conservative, powerful and moralistic of Church figures in twentieth-century Ireland. And adding one irony to another, the Church's influence in education, long held as the conditioning influence of the population at large, is waning because it can no longer afford to maintain the influential position it was given by the state.

The most prominent events displaying how things have moved on were Taoiseach Enda Kenny's withering rebuke (Dáil 20 July 2011) to Rome because of their lame reaction to the report on child abuse in the Diocese of Cloyne and Dublin and the decision to close the Irish Embassy in the Vatican City. Whether for financial or other reasons it is clear that changed days have arrived, Ireland's relationship with the Vatican is at an all-time low and any subsequent political talk of reviewing this decision seems to put such a possibility on the 'long-finger'.

I stress that in saying the above I am totally respectful of people's right to articulate their personal faith in the denomination or sect of their choice or outside the denominations. For the purposes of this book however, it is important to say that right across Ireland all people of faith and none can live without fear of the many negatives of old religious battles: for many religion is now in its rightful place, in the personal realm, and Article 44 of the Irish Constitution reflects this. I therefore feel that the old religious arguments against unity have gone away. In mentioning Article 44, it is perhaps with a little irony that there may be more of a debate about the explicit reference to God, which those of no particular religious faith feel rather excludes the sizeable group of Irish non-believers.

I personally hope that ultimately in a united Ireland, while religious and other labels will remain important to people, the label 'citizen' will have its maximum importance and relevance. Not that it should dilute those other parts of people's identity but should rather be inclusive in the true republican sense, thus rendering Catholic, Protestant, Dissenter, Muslim, people of all faiths and none, immigrant and members of all other groups as totally equal.

Chapter Eight

Achieving a United Ireland

I planned and started this chapter forty-eight hours before the 2011 Irish presidential election polling day. One of the candidates, Sean Gallagher, has just had a torrid time. The last of the TV presidential debates among the seven candidates has just taken place on an RTE programme called the *Frontline* hosted by presenter Pat Kenny. Gallagher was topping the polls, well ahead of the field, much to the surprise of many and obvious anger of some of his competitors. The pressure was on him not to slip on any late 'banana skins'. One of the two main areas on which he was continually challenged was his membership of and association with Fianna Fáil which, as noted earlier, suffered a massive setback in the Irish general election in February 2011: they were regularly described as 'toxic' by many commentators in an obvious alignment with the 'toxic' banks, so Gallagher had, while acknowledging his former membership of Fianna Fáil, insisted he was now running as 'an independent' candidate, and thereby minimised his FF party involvement.

Enter Martin McGuinness, the Sinn Féin presidential candidate, who had temporarily stood aside as Deputy First Minister in the Belfast Assembly to mount his campaign for President in the South. During the *Frontline* programme, McGuinness challenged Sean Gallagher about his involvement in a €5000 per-head Fianna Fáil fundraising dinner with the former party leader and Taoiseach Brian Cowan in attendance. The Sinn

Féiner said he had spoken to a man that very evening who claimed he had given Sean Gallagher a cheque for €5000, therefore depicting the supposedly 'independent' candidate as a 'Fianna Fáil bagman' who was, it seems, not being totally open and honest with the public. Gallagher immediately said 'Not true!', but twenty minutes later into the programme and after being repeatedly pressed on the issue, he conceded that this 'could have happened' but that he couldn't specifically recollect this, and that there 'could have been an envelope' given to him. His choice of words had disturbing political connotations, given the alleged 'brown envelope' culture of Irish politics in general and of Fianna Fáil in particular. The following morning he still couldn't satisfactorily clarify the matter during a radio interview, again with Pat Kenny.

It was one of those crucial moments. To those bored or disillusioned with politics it was just more of the same; middle-aged, and older, politicians vying for position by going for the jugular at the expense of the more important issues. But to political anoraks, party hacks and the media this was 'blood sport' at its best. McGuinness—who had had his own negative run-ins with the press—suddenly became their 'darling': he had carried out a metaphorical 'knee-capping'; it was interrogation, which he was well used to; he had delivered the bullet; he had flashed those steely eyes; other colourful descriptions were used. Suddenly his oft-reviled paramilitary past provided the media with the supposedly smart metaphors upon which Gallagher was hanged.

But what did this incident really show, and why do I recount this particular incident?

Sinn Féin had entered the presidential race and chosen their high-profile candidate with a specific purpose. That purpose was not actually to win the contest - a highly-unlikely outcome under the circumstances - but rather to increase their political currency and vote record in the South, mostly at the expense of the hapless Fianna Fáil. Sinn Féin had their eyes on the longer-term future and wanted to attract former Fianna Fáil votes. Increasing their vote in the South in a meaningful way had been a hard nut for Sinn Féin to crack. They did not get a 'peace process bounce' as expected in the South during the early/mid 2000s, but their February 2011 result was good. Now that a large segment of Irish voters was seriously disillusioned with Fianna Fáil, an effective presidential campaign would be another feather in the SF political cap.

120

As it all turned out, McGuinness's claim had a massive impact. Support for Sean Gallagher suffered a catastrophic reversal, with the near-complete transfer of his lead to the eventual winner, Michael D Higgins. The claim by the Sinn Féin man, however, had as many holes in it as Gallagher's bungled responses. So, in effect, an unsubstantiated claim fuelled by media running on a fictitious 'tweet' in the middle of the *Frontline* programme provided yet another example of Sinn Féin turning on what was now their 'nearest opponent' in the South, Fianna Fáil.

Outlining this bit of political theatre surrounding Gallagher and McGuinness serves to remind us of politicians' propensity to sacrifice the 'broader picture' or the 'longer view' for short-term personal-or-political advantage. Martin McGuinness neither increased the party percentage of the vote by any substantial margin nor did he particularly gain from the Fianna Fáil stable. It had an effect, yes, but this was far from the overall strategy behind the campaign. Yet, knowing the party political psyche, I can imagine the hero worship response of many Sinn Féiners to McGuinness's role in changing the course of the election. I agree with Odran Flynn (*Irish* Times 1 Nov 2011) that McGuinness's now-famous intervention was only a pyrrhic victory: for not only did the intervention fail in bringing Fianna Fáilers to the Sinn Féin stable, but it also solidified the remaining Fianna Fáil vote to Sean Gallagher, as he still came second in the election relatively well ahead of McGuinness.

This type of blindness is not new, nor is one such incident proof of the point. But as I have already spoken in detail of 'the curse of the nearest opponent' it is clear that I have concerns about political parties being the *only* main drivers for a united Ireland. Their short-termism, their fear of the nearest opponent and, on the broader front, their arguably-questionable commitment to the ideal of unity itself, delivers a serious challenge to the rest of us. As if it wasn't already hard enough to win the Northern vote to achieve this aim, we have to deal with this particular plague on the Nationalist/Republican political house.

I therefore believe that an important part of the drive for a united Ireland will have to come from *outside* the party system, but it will of course influence and include the players in that system. The parties need a substantial outside organisation in terms of personnel and finance to be a conduit and provide the space for parties to focus on this project without the direct baggage of negative party posturing and positioning.

This space is where parties come together for the exclusively longer view, leaving short-term battles to other places and on other subjects so that they do not impinge on the broader aim of uniting the nation.

It is hard to prescribe what exactly such an organisation will look like and who the main players will be, but I would be very satisfied if this book prompted some of that debate. I do envisage high-profile Irish and Irish diaspora figures; those with a genuine commitment to uniting the nation; academics, thinkers and those with economic abilities; people who are very politically aware - maybe some with previous party connections but who are absolutely prepared to transcend personal and political differences and work with all parties and people for this common goal. In other words, any such organisation would be high-powered, visionary and politically strong; for convenience I will call this potential body 'Vision Ireland'.

I appreciate that parties have already made some proposals in this general direction: Sinn Féin has its ongoing campaign; the SDLP has published its paper on unity; Fianna Fáil declares its long-term commitment and so on. But years pass by without serious concerted effort and vision, and really meaningful work on the practicalities is still lacking. We have now had long enough to see what real change looks like; the Good Friday Agreement has been ushered in with its positives and negatives, including the largely-ineffective North-South bodies. So, as we live through the decade of key commemorations of important centenary dates new opportunities exist to broaden and deepen the conversation within Ireland, and internationally, on crucial related issues.

Now is the time to demonstrate with conviction and real action that we can put forward substance and detail, over aspiration and generality!

I am therefore outlining some important contextual issues that Vision Ireland could engage with to further the work of uniting Ireland. In essence the role of Vision Ireland would involve putting cogent arguments forward in detail, in reports and in the media, convening where needed focus groups, symposia and conferences: all three vehicles will include civic society representatives and politicians when appropriate. This work will be both on national and international fronts and include the following steps.

Economy

I readily admit writing a book on this topic in recessionary times is contrarian to say the least, but economics will of course be of central importance to the debate. I believe Vision Ireland could commission professional papers on economic best approaches to a united Ireland, and these could be presented in full detail but also, I stress again, in a form for general-purpose reference by the public and media. Such a professional approach would far outweigh my contributions, but I will still refer to the following.

I have already said that the North does not have an economy in the real sense. Its receipt of the London cheque, distribution within government departments, low Foreign Direct Investment (FDI) success rates, its inability to make real economic decisions, including tax rates and even basic retention of tax revenue raised in the North, means Northern Ireland is a highly-restricted financial entity. This cannot continue indef-initely. High Northern reliance on public sector jobs financed by England is already being curtailed, and even relatively small cut-backs have caused considerable consternation. If this continues in the long-term the prognosis is not good, especially if the British Chancellor's proposal to introduce regional public-sector pay rates becomes a reality for Northern Ireland. Quite clearly, this measure could lead to longer-term pay freezes for the public service sector, with the ripple effect of even less economic activity across the area.

Comment is made on the importance of the 'knowledge economy' in the North, but where, for example, was the drive to maximise cloud computing possibilities? Is the rather blunt education system in the North ever going to be flexible enough to educate the community to meaningfully build the knowledge economy? Can they afford the step-up in Research and Development (R&D) to not only play catch-up but to evolve in this fast-changing world? Can Ulster-Irish tourism ever be maximised when Northern authorities still impose a mental 'border' on much of their marketing? At a very local level, can some Unionists ever accept that cultural tourism is not really 'successful' in a literal sense, when they are claiming high visitor numbers to twelfth of July festivals which are, in the main, made up of the families and supporters of participants? There is a drastic need for a higher vision.

In short, decades of high public service employment and a corresponding lack of vision and experience in entrepreneurial work, with some laudable exceptions, combined with longstanding partitionist attitudes even towards basic tourism, means that Northern Ireland (as it stands today) has little if any chance of ever 'making a profit'. Even if it were to generate more money than the block grant currently received from London, it would still not constitute a self-sufficient financial entity. We must accept that industrialised Great Britain, its political élite and the political masters in the North have failed to deliver a successful Northern Ireland economy, and one cannot just blame 'the Troubles'. Decades of decline in traditional industries in the North preceding 'the Troubles' were not replaced by similar advances in GB during that period, and the present 'open economy' of Britain is a polar opposite to that in the North.

Vision Ireland could therefore co-ordinate the case for maximising all economic activity such as Foreign Direct Investment (FDI), indigenous businesses, funding for Research and Development (R&D) and for what is often referred to as 'the all-Ireland economy'. Vision Ireland could also rebut the usual 'cost-of-the-North' argument by outlining the amount of tax revenue that is *not* retained in Belfast, which, in a united Ireland, would be channelled back into the new economy. Those who proffer the rather restricted arguments about the North's economy should be confronted with the bigger debate rather than the very limited one that has been the case up to now.

I also think that Vision Ireland could introduce specific ideas on special international bonds, alliances and relationships that could underpin a fledgling, all-Ireland economy. I have no doubt that the Irish diaspora would do their best in helping with the chance to unite the Irish nation. Investing in what many of the diaspora want would be a very practical statement of intent behind real support for the new paradigm. In addition, outlining ways of maximising the benefits of economic links with the diaspora could be another project for Vision Ireland, and I acknowledge that various efforts are already being made on this task.

But we should not only rely on the Irish diaspora in what will be a twenty-first century of change. The economic powerhouses of this century are already being built, and we have to think 'outside the box' to deliver an economic model that delivers for Ireland. The BRIC countries (Brazil, Russia, India and China) are the new drivers; they have already established a broad network of countries and alliances to work and trade with. Vision Ireland could engage in some 'blue-sky' thinking and action that builds relationships with some or all of the BRIC countries that consequently delivers maximum economic co-operation as a gateway to Europe and beyond. This includes business, educational and cultural alliances that yield jobs, student exchanges and research projects. In addition, and within the context of unity, consideration should be given as to how special bonds could raise money from the BRIC countries and help the new all-Ireland fledgling economy.

It is interesting to note in this context that planning permission for the first phase of the Europe-China Trading Hub in Athlone has been granted. Buyers from Europe and the US will be able to source Chinese goods there. The completed project is estimated to cover over 300 acres and is a Chinese-backed development to the tune of €1.4 billion (*Irish Times* 3 December 2011). In his December 2011 budget, Michael Noonan, Fine Gael Minister for Finance, introduced a foreign-earnings deduction scheme for those spending 60 days a year in the BRIC countries and South Africa, in an effort to expand business in those regions (Dáil Budget speech 6 December 2011). But perhaps an even greater sign for future relationships was the February 2012 visit to Ireland by Xi Jinping, the man seen as the next in line to be China's leader. Tourism, trade and China seeing Ireland as a 'foothold' into the wider European market were all on the agenda (*Irish Times* 7 & 18 February 2012) and further measures were agreed when Taoiseach Enda Kenny paid a return visit to China (*Irish Independent*, 28 March 2012).

In anticipation of some typically-negative reaction to these new ideas, I have to say that we cannot afford—at this point in our history—what I call 'dreary steeple' thinking militating against 'blue-sky' or new thinking on this project. We need to be brave and determined in our approaches.

In the debate on economics, Unionists nearly always ignore the people who pay the bills for Northern Ireland, namely the English tax-payer. It's a rather ungrateful approach to those who have paid for the North for decades. Should opinions from those English tax-payers be sought in this ever-changing context? The UK returned to recession after a second quarter (Jan-Mar 2012) of economic contraction (*BBC* report online 25 April 2012 'UK Economy in double-dip recession'), public services are being cut and there is talk of tight fiscal restraints in the UK for at least another decade. Do the people who pay the bill for Northern Ireland have any thoughts about continuing this practice in what is, relatively speaking, difficult economic times for them too? The English tax-payer is contributing to each Northern Irish person some three times more than he/she is getting back. I therefore think that Vision Ireland could have a role within its economics work focusing on the GB sector and assessing the mood of the people on this matter, rather than pursuing the usual diet of vested political interest and agendas.

Constitutional Change

The Union of Great Britain and Northern Ireland is changing. I therefore feel there are very important conversations to take place as this change evolves; these can inform Vision Ireland's work, perhaps even yielding specific projects for that organisation.

The regions of the Union, namely England, Scotland, Wales and Northern Ireland, are distinctly different in their views of themselves and each other compared with even a decade ago. Wales is perhaps the least changed in this regard as its regional assembly has limited powers. England on the other hand is possibly more nationalistic than at any time in the modern era, but the Scottish Parliament has most definitely been a catalyst for radical change with some 49 per cent declaring support for Scottish independence (*Reuters* report online 16 October 2011 'UK-Scotland-Independence'). A referendum on the issue has been promised by Alex Salmond, First Minister of Scotland and leader of the Scottish National Party (SNP) and is scheduled to take place in 2014. The questions to appear on the ballot paper still have to be confirmed, but many pundits say that Scotland will be at least the closest thing to independent, if not actually independent.

The implications for the Union, and therefore our situation in Ireland, are immense.

Scottish independence would render change for the UK on both the international front and obviously within the Union itself. London will want to avoid the big losses to its international standing and will, I believe, pressurise the people of Scotland on many domestic issues to protect that standing. The stakes are high. Is it possible that the UK could lose its permanent seat on the United Nations Security Council to one of the emerging countries? If so that would be a political shift of immense proportions for this once strong empire! Even if what has become known as 'devo max' (full fiscal autonomy) is the outcome for Scotland, I believe substantial change will still occur. Will 'devo max' mean that Scotland is totally responsible for its relationship with the EU and other international organisations? Will it mean that the formula for financial support of the UK regions (whatever will be in place at the time) is rendered useless? Will the kinship of Scotland to Ireland in general and northern Unionists in particular further change the attitudes of the latter to London?

This potential for change became the main issue that Britain's retiring senior civil servant Gus O'Donnell addressed in his final speech as cabinet secretary (*Daily Mail* report online 22 Dec 2011). O'Donnell was of the firm belief that the Union may not survive the pressure for Scottish independence in the coming years. A senior 'non-political' voice articulating this opinion is very noteworthy and my own views also found resonance with Paul Gillespie's when he suggested that the implication for Unionists, particularly in Northern Ireland, could be great. Gillespie asks the important rhetorical question: in a changed UK, would Northern Irelanders' slight identification with an England-dominated successor state, not weaken further? Gillespie correctly refers to social research that displays an ever-widening gap between the political identities in the UK, particularly those with a strong and rising English identity (*Irish Times* 24 Dec. 2011). And we have to accept that increasing numbers of English are seriously examining, some would say wanting, an exclusive English state, which would of course spell the end of the UK.

The reaction of some within Unionism to the evolving Scottish question has been very illuminating. Perhaps most disturbing of all was the response of Reg Empey, former Ulster Unionist party leader, in a speech delivered in the House of Lords. Put bluntly it was incredulous, worse still I think it was dangerous. Empey said that if Scottish nationalists got their way "it could possibly reignite the difficulties ['the Troubles'] we have just managed to overcome". He went on to say that if Scottish independence was gained, Northern Ireland would have "a foreign country on one side of us and a foreign country on the other side of us", therefore ending up "like West Pakistan" (*News Letter*, 27 Jan. 2012).

With 'tongue firmly in cheek' I have to ask: if Scotland were to become a 'foreign country' overnight, what does that say for the 'special historical link' with that nation and the Ulster-Scots relationship? In addition—and yet again—we have a geographical third of Ulster and a sizeable section of Northern Irish citizens declared 'foreign' as well! But most seriously of all is the main point of Empey's argument, that is, the underpinning threat of violence from whatever quarter. What happened to the commitment to peaceful methods? At a very early stage of the Scottish debate we have a Northern Irish politician resorting to the old tactic. If change comes there will be a violent reaction, in other words the status-quo has, once again, to be protected by the menace of violence. Of course, if such violence were to occur, Reg Empey would no doubt recline on his red benches well removed from the 'grubby streets'. There will be much more to come on the Scottish question and its implications.

The British Royal family, for so long the important bastion of Protestant succession for many Protestants in the North, will now allow members to marry Roman Catholics without affecting their right to the throne. This step into the twentieth century (Yes, I did mean the twentieth!) will perhaps one day be added to by a step into the twenty-first century, by disestablishing the Church of England, thus leaving future queens and kings free to be Roman Catholic, or any other religion, and taking sectarianism out of the royal family once and for all. This would further weaken the Protestant element of traditional links to Great Britain and, while acknowledging that not all of that faith in Northern Ireland has this as their number-one issue, there are still quite a number who regard the religion issue as very important. It is interesting to note that DUP MP Jeffrey Donaldson and some party colleagues actually marched to Downing Street protesting against the move permitting British kings and queens to marry Roman Catholics (*Irish News* 23 Nov. 2011)!

Europe/EU

Another bigger-picture issue is the relationship with 'Europe' (i.e. the EU). Writing in the context of uncertainty is difficult; conjecture about the future of the Euro and the nature of EU bodies is rife, and in an uncertain world the media headline too often has a greater effect than the substance behind it. However, assuming there will be an EU not considerably dissimilar to the present day, and perhaps even more federalist in structure, the probable debate will be as follows: If the UK has its two main players, i.e. England and Scotland, largely pressing their own agendas in Europe, what does that mean for Northern Ireland? Many of us know that the North has not been well served by the 'mother' government's role in Brussels. Through my university work on a European-based project and my role as an MLA, I have direct experience of how little the North has worked the Brussels system to its own benefit. The availability of 'peace money' has disguised the ineffective role played in recent years by the Westminster machinery, especially the Northern Ireland Office (NIO), and more recently, the Office of the First Minister & Deputy First Minister (OFMDFM). In contrast, the South has benefited considerably from its EU membership due largely to the effectiveness of a strong Dublin team who work within the EU. Even hard-headed Northern Irish business people have openly admitted this to me when I was on a study visit to Brussels.

If this deficit continues, the North will largely be standing still in terms of meaningful, effective representation in the EU – and the corresponding lack of material gain. The North has far more in common with the South of Ireland, and I believe that if Ireland went to Brussels as one united entity rather than the Belfast administration going as an appendage of industrial GB, the needs of the North would be much more effectively met. Even with Dublin's difficult relationship in the midst of massive bail-outs and a tarnished image, it is clear that they are adopting a policy aimed at regaining their prestige in the EU and eventually getting back to 'business as usual', a scenario in which the Dublin politicians and officials in Brussels have so-far, performed well.

Now, if we add to that scenario the little-Englander performance by British PM David Cameron at the all-important EU summit (8-9 Dec. 2011), when he vetoed an EU strategy to assist Euro recovery, we could have interesting days ahead. Representatives from Belfast and Edinburgh criticised Cameron's approach, but why would they be surprised at him 'running solo' without any substantial reference to the other regions of the UK? The stark truth is that Tory backbenchers' and little-Englanders' socio-political aims will always be more important than Northern Ireland interests.

How it will all play out is difficult to tell. Some say that the UK is protecting its financial services industry (if it does not impose a financial transaction tax it will remain a strong hub for related industries); while others think that increased isolation from Europe could cost the UK dearly. I would be more of the Eddie Hobbs' school of thought, arguing that there could be solid opportunities for Ireland here, and a 'new plank for recovery' could be opening up (*Sunday Independent*, 11 Dec. 2011). If so, the North would have another reason to increase its EU effectiveness by going to Brussels as one with the rest of Ireland. However, I do appreciate that too much of the Unionist attitude towards Europe has been shaped by very narrow British media and political attitudes: the old tabloid rallying call to 'save the British sausage' was a metaphor for this type of insularity, something that would have to be countered in a much more professional and informed manner if the North is ever to free itself from the effects of these, and other such regressive attitudes.

Opinion in the South

I was once struck by the comments of a Dublin commentator (I cannot remember the name) when he spoke about former President Mary McAleese coming to Dublin in the late seventies to work in the media. Mary would regularly speak about a united Ireland, and the commentator remarked that many in that particular Dublin circle had already given up on that idea. The reason for this he said, was the PIRA campaign of violence. Such was the public resentment and embarrassment associated with that campaign, any sympathy for the earlier years of defending the Catholic community had dissolved. So, in the minds of many in the South, violent republicans were in actual fact harming popular support for unity.

Yet despite this understandable undercurrent of ill-feeling, all the main parties in the South accept the ideal of unity and how it can come about within the Good Friday Agreement context. In addition, and despite a modest decline, popular support for unity in the South still exceeded 50 per cent in Oct 2010 and July 2011 (politics.ie). Therefore, I think the idea of national reconciliation through unity should remain the subject of focused, forward-thinking efforts that will foster enthusiasm among the ambivalent, and re-consolidate the idea of unity among supportive others. This can happen in context of the debate on the 'second republic' and related economic improvements, during the 2012-2022 decade of commemorations. This scenario will render many opportunities for Vision Ireland to engage with politicians, civic society and the public at large.

Opinion in the North

Vision Ireland's work in the North will of course be different; this is the very heart of the Good Friday Agreement consent principle. However, I believe that with some of the completed research and preparation work I referred to above, engagement can take place with politicians, the voluntary and community sectors and the broader general public. I can foresee a publicity campaign outlining the main principles for the case of unity followed up by direct engagement with all the sectors. There is no sense trying to engage unless you are going with something of substance on the economic, identity and cultural fronts.

Having reasonably well-worked proposals put in a non-threatening way is, for me, central to the future of the unity debate in the North. When people advocate a united Ireland they are correctly challenged with the argument that 'nobody has yet outlined what it would look like or how it would work'. Therefore, the abstract has to be left behind and we must start to outline the reality. What I have tried to do in this chapter and the next is map out a way that counters that argument, gives something of the potential reality, and hopefully leads to an informed debate on national unity.

This work throughout Ireland cannot be the preserve of one or more political parties. But it follows that a body of the type of Vision Ireland would have to constructively work with political parties of all hues throughout Ireland and beyond. It would need to be made clear from the outset therefore, that Vision Ireland would not be a threat to these political parties, and would not be in a position to interfere in other areas of political activity. Vision Ireland would have to explain the essence of its work, that is, to be a conduit for constructive ideas towards unity, whereby efforts must be complementary, not adversarial, and where space is given to the various parties free from the normal rub of party politics.

Strategy Template

The following does not give a detailed strategy, but I do feel that even by outlining this broad four-step approach I can show readers there is logic to the process and therefore value to the overall idea and approach.

The initial stage would be the all-important professional research and presentation work on the many economic issues for successful unity. Next would come reports on the constitutional, social and political aspects of culture-and-identity issues, and thirdly, the specifics of the proposed approaches for garnering local and international support. The import of this work cannot be underestimated and fully explains my earlier point that Vision Ireland should be high-powered and well resourced. While some might scoff at this type of proposal—especially in its early theoretical stage—history and experience shows that the scoffing soon abates once some real substance comes out of such work.

The second stage could proceed quite quickly because minimal research is required. This stage is outlining and implementing the approaches within GB. That is, getting opinions from the general public and politicians on their financial contribution to Northern Ireland and the future of the Union. This is straightforward but very important work.

The third stage would be the considerable international work on garnering political, economic and popular support among the diaspora and the BRIC countries as outlined earlier. This would require high-powered approaches and negotiation, again demonstrating the need for a Vision Ireland of substance. If successful to any reasonable degree these endeavours could change the entire architecture of this project. In a challenging twenty-first century a strong viable economic framework is a very attractive proposition. Post 'IMF Ireland'—hopefully with a drastically re-scheduled debt provision — and a straight-jacketed North have to look to a very different financial future. (For an excellent article on the impact of re-working the promissory notes system for the Irish debt level, see Simon Carswell *Irish Times* 30 January 2012.)

With those three stages largely completed, or at least yielding enough information and proposals to move forwards, the fourth and final stage would be the extensive groundwork in Ireland. Detailed tactics and timing would of course be for others to plan and implement; there will always be general and specific approaches to this opinion-forming work amongst the public. One feeds the other and it would be up to Vision Ireland to implement its programme, employing tactics and timing to maximum effect. The evidence from the research, and international and GB-related work could be used in general publicity, for informing the political conversation, and then specifically within particular social, educational or business sectors. This is where the weight of the Irish diaspora would be brought to bear in an international setting. The population throughout Ireland is at a place where they will no longer be swayed by the old clichés. The detailed experiences of the lead-up to the Good Friday Agreement, and all the subsequent stumbles and advances have provided important lessons for us all. When allied to the drastically-changed positions of many of the political parties, we can see that Irish society has certainly been transformed, and is evolving and progressing from the old zero-sum political-slogans game. In addition, the politics of the financial meltdown and the grotesque bank situation have also delivered many lessons to the people in the South. So my strong view at this stage is that the people will listen to the detail if it is fairly and squarely put to them.

We must never underestimate the capacity for change, by people who have been through the mill of difficulty!

The above is only a template giving a pointer to the different types of work that are required and the order in which they could be pursued. This type of approach can potentially move the debate away from banal calls for a united Ireland which are so easily rejected. As we go into the decade of commemoration, such banality must give way to substance.

Chapter Nine

Final Thoughts

In 1972 the late Fine Gael leader and Taoiseach Dr Garrett Fitzgerald penned the following (*Towards a New Ireland*, Torc Books, 176):

> *I believe the time has come for all Irish politicians who genuinely believe in a united Ireland, so organised that people from both communities will feel equally at home within it, to speak out and to lead the people of Ireland towards this goal.*

A lot of very troubled water has passed under the bridge since then, but we must remember that Ireland in 1972 was in the middle of deeply troubled waters; continuing the metaphor one could say a political-and-social tsunami had already hit the island. So Fitzgerald was neither, writing in easy times nor at an academic distance. He articulated a very informed political and personal opinion.

Of course, as 'the Troubles' went from one terrible stage to another, opinions changed. The legacy was not only death and destruction but also a series of emotional and psychological barriers to full inter-party communication about how such a catastrophe could happen in the first place, and how it could ultimately be resolved. Violence, condemnation of violence, and prolonged differences between those who did-or-did-not pursue violence, became the benchmarks for political discussion for years to come.

Subsequently, the Good Friday Agreement became a vehicle for other types of 'creative ambiguity'. For those who did not want to think beyond partition, the Good Friday Agreement was THE final settlement, the endgame had been reached. One example of this understanding was when former Taoiseach John Bruton spoke of "at last" reaching a "political accommodation between unionism and nationalism on this island" (*Irish Times* 11 Nov 2011). Bruton goes on to say—in the context of commemorating the centenary of 1916—that nothing should be said or done "that would put that very recent reconciliation of Unionism and Nationalism at risk". People can and will interpret things differently but I think Bruton's words reveal an attitude of 'job done' and 'endgame reached'. The Good Friday Agreement is also a convenient way for some of putting that dreadful 'northern sectarian' trouble to bed. Yet, thirteen years after the GFA, even Professor Ronan Fanning of University College Dublin would still describe the North as a "dysfunctional entity" (*Sunday Independent* 6 Nov 2011). A very political statement such as that neither sits easily with a narrative saying Northern Ireland was a totally sectarian problem, nor one of a 'job done'.

I very firmly believe the central problem of the North was deeply political, premised on partition and how it was shaped in socio-political terms by that partition.

But we are now in changed days. The once fragile peace process has sufficiently deepened as to be reasonably consolidated. Virtually everyone will say they do not want to go back to the 'bad old days', but we are occasionally reminded—particularly by dissident republicans— that some still do. Despite this and some loyalist paramilitaries also engaging in violent acts, I believe that deep-rooted change has taken place at various levels, but there is still a requirement for a political debate. The North is still deeply divided; it is still a place apart; it still does not have enough shared ambition (something I don't believe it can ever have in its current form), and it remains as I described earlier embroiled in a democratic stand-off. Taoiseach Enda Kenny may have said there is no schedule for a unified Ireland (*Irish Times*, 29 March 2012), which might be another way of trying to put the difficult issue on the very long finger. However, I believe we can debate and move forward all the related issues during the decade of commemorations of key events from 1912-22. This is an ideal time for deeper political conversation in a peaceful context and in a non-threatening manner.

In addition to the key centenary dates, former Presbyterian Moderator Norman Hamilton is correct to remind us (*Irish Times* 15 Nov 2011) that 2018 will be the fiftieth anniversary of what is generally regarded as the key 1968 date of the start of 'the Troubles'. Many people might recoil in horror because of our propensity to look backwards to anniversaries. I, on the other hand, would be a 'glass half full' person in this regard: I look upon this particular date as an additional opportunity to set aside the rather surface-level debates about 'the Troubles', given their direct lineage from partition. I would therefore welcome constructive engagement, rather than the tragic but incomplete league-table-of-killings approach which avoids so many important issues, including the role of the state. I also think that if we handle the important 2012, 2013, 2014 and 2016 dates correctly, there are several opportunities to learn from *real* history, and not from contrived histories that are read retrospectively through whichever partisan lens suits best.

I purposely decided to produce this book early in this important decade in the hope that it will make a real contribution, in a timely way. I have supplied a reasonable amount of detail on my personal experiences so as to inform the reader of where I am coming from. My educational, historical, social and political questioning has led me to the profound belief that ultimately Ireland will be stronger 'as one'. It is certainly not a surface belief, it is held in the knowledge and experience of many harsh realities. One of the current harsh realities is the recession, and difficult and problematic as it might be for us all, we cannot let it stifle this important debate. There has been a propensity in the past to allow 'difficult times' to impede the debate on Irish unity: for example, the Second World War, the fiftieth anniversary of the Easter Rising, and 'the Troubles' have all been used as excuses for inaction. We cannot, and should not add the current recession to that list. Despite the uncertainties, commentator Paul Cullen is already prepared to talk of economic sovereignty possibly returning to Ireland by 2016 (*Irish Times* 22 Nov.2011), and the Irish Business and Employers' Confederation (IBEC) proposes that the number employed in the private sector, excluding construction, will return to 'pre-crisis' levels, also by 2016. So, there will be life after the recession; therefore we should get on with the required work.

Key to that work is the creation of the body I called 'Vision Ireland'. If we could get the right people with reasonable resources, this body could put a lot of the detail to the many building-blocks of this work by co-ordinating the efforts of individuals and organisations. It would combine Irish and international work, always maintaining that blend of the bigger and smaller pictures. It would give standing and weight to the project, which will not be delivered by any single political party. I stress again this is not to criticise anyone for articulating their particular views. However, considering the breadth of all those sectors we need to respectfully speak with, drives me to the conclusion that Vision Ireland, as broadly outlined in this book, could work credibly with diverse audiences while giving sufficient space to existing political parties to work on the central ideal without the burden of their day-to-day differences and agendas.

There are many key sectors and issues to be addressed. The debate must be given much more focus and raised far above the generalities that bedevil it. I have already addressed many of these issues as the book progressed, however, I would like to add the following remarks.

The Irish diaspora has a major role to play. While many Irish don't like the distance that emigration has caused, there is sometimes a benefit to informed opinion coming from a relatively-objective distance, particularly when it is underpinned by respected and committed people whose network is both expansive and influential. This influence would be even stronger when working in unison with the Irish at home! The work in GB that I referred to is also important, as it has often been an ignored voice controlled by the 'political élite' to serve their agenda. That control has to be transcended. Let us see what a more general, informed and unbridled opinion might be.

In Ireland there are two major areas that need to be addressed. Firstly, assessing and informing general opinion in the South, and secondly, the crucial debate with northern Protestants. I believe the former will not respond well to the prospect of any one political entity or group putting forward their own limited political arguments. Again, this is where I see the strength of Vision Ireland which, with the standing of committed personnel and professionalism, will have a greater chance of 'being heard' on the issue of unity. This will not be easy work, but I believe that even those people who have settled into regarding the Irish state as 'complete' as it is, will respond to cogent arguments that sensibly draw from the taproot of the Irish nation. This will not be about jingoism; it will be about substance on many issues, especially economics and socio-cultural policies. I should add that there will also be some work among the nationalists in the North. Many of the arguments that will be put forward to people in the South will also be of help with this group.

Moving to the northern Protestant/Unionist community, I have made various points in this book that perhaps challenge that community, but I have done so respectfully and on the basis that I too have roots in that community. Those points may generally be summed up by saying that I don't believe that the North can ever become a normal democratic entity. The manner in which it came into being and its subsequent dreadful record for nearly eight decades have seen to that. The North hasn't got an economy in any real sense; it depends on England for its finances and its engagement with the EU (and all other international organisations and issues). Furthermore, a massive section of the North's media influence is London-based, providing a cultural and social outlook that many unionists feel distant from. Political claims of allegiance to Britain that were made to reinforce the artificial separation from the rest of Ireland do not render the North 'the same as Finchley'. The history of the northern Protestants is inextricably linked to four concentrated centuries and more of living, working and contributing to Ireland; the Orange and Masonic Orders, the main Protestant churches and many sporting organisations are 'all-Ireland' in nature. So, ever since partition, it is clear that claims of so-called 'Britishness' by Northern Protestants have, on many occasions, been rooted more in localised socio-political antipathies, rather than being a positive and genuine embrace of GB values and social cohesion.

But those of us who want a united Ireland must now take the opportunity of this decade of commemorations to open meaningful engagement with the Northern Protestants. Let us remember this is not a homogenous group. Politically there are already some who would welcome unity, and then, as we move through the rest of that continuum of people, we will find opinions of various strengths, and hopefully, various levels of support.

In advocating such engagement I think it is also essential to anticipate the negative arguments of those I have described as the 'dreary steeple' thinkers, who continue to perpetrate the pessimistic view that a united Ireland will never happen. I have lived long enough to hear that

Stormont would never change; that the police would never change; that the Unionists would never change; that 'the Troubles' would never end; that ceasefires would never happen; that an agreement would never be made; that the DUP would never share power with Sinn Féin... and so on. That list of 'never, never, never' could of course be added to. But I think I have made the point; change comes when the will for change exists. It will therefore be important that Vision Ireland approaches the numerous difficult issues in professional, respectful and positive ways, with a mind to all the subtleties, sensitivities and nuances involved; the type of body I foresee Vision Ireland being would be more than capable of doing that.

DUP leader and First Minister Peter Robinson made a speech at his party's 2011 conference advocating a 'united community' in the North, hoping that an increasing number of northern Catholics would be content in the United Kingdom and even vote for the DUP. Of course, one would therefore expect him to hope that they would also then vote *against* a united Ireland in a referendum. Peter Robinson obviously realises that bringing the Catholic population on board is important, perhaps essential, to the project of keeping the North within the UK. Most importantly of all, he described missing the current 'opportunity' of building this united northern society within the UK in the following manner:

> *Miss it and we may miss it for ever. Miss it and we may drift and stray* (*Irish Times* 28 Nov. 2011).

I believe, not just because of these words alone, that the debate on the future of the North in the Ireland of the future is 'on', even within the minds of Northern Unionists. Robinson's words reveal they have reached a junction, knowing that what went before in the North cannot be sustained. So where does Northern Unionism go now? Can Peter Robinson and the larger Unionist community really be satisfied with a so-called 'united community' in the North that has no real political power; no real economy; and no sustainable sense of unified self-identity because of all the aforementioned cracks in that 'unity'? And how, one might ask, would any such society cope or adapt in any meaningful way in our fast changing world?

I readily admit it is easier to defend the status-quo. The harder work is for those, like me, who advocate change. But as people sensibly and professionally argue for that change, the reception within elements of the Unionist community and the more general civic community may be more reflective and positive than one would initially imagine. It is clear that Peter Robinson has at least already reflected on the issue, although admittedly from his own side of the debate. But nevertheless, the conversation has definitely begun.

My points to the Unionist community are therefore as follows:

In a changing British union, devolution of very-limited powers to Belfast leaves Unionists in a legislative and constitutional limbo. The Belfast administration can do very little, and the broader UK picture is one of political contraction. I believe the 'little Englander' approach will steadily increase, and the North's reliance on the English cheque book will come under greater political and economic strain. If the Union itself comes under increasing pressure because of the Scottish question, and Britain becomes more isolated in Europe, I have no doubt that Northern interests will suffer in a more pronounced manner. Of course the North trades with GB, as does the South, but links with the larger world trading blocs from within the European bloc are becoming much more important in this century. The 2011/12 debate about the UK's place in Europe could have long-lasting effects for all of us in Ireland. Cameron's 'little England' card may yet prove very important to the entire debate on what exactly Unionism is – and what the future holds. Do Northern Unionists really have a future in an increasingly-fractured Britain?

As I said earlier in the book, some twenty years ago a Dubliner spoke to me of 'leap-frogging over London to Berlin' to conduct business. He wasn't saying that he didn't do some business in England, but he was also benefiting from the European potential. There may be serious difficulties in Europe at the time of writing this book, but I am confident that we will come out of those travails and Ireland will maximise its own position, while also seriously observing and examining the possibility of the UK's increasing isolation in Europe.

I think Northern Unionists should also seriously observe and examine these possibilities. I feel they should challenge themselves about the 'benefits' of linking with GB if the main benefit is forever going to be the block grant, an amount forever decided on by London. If London constantly, in relative terms, gives less, while simultaneously expecting more income and growth from within the very restricted entity that the

North currently is, then where does this take us? The North would become increasingly disenfranchised and isolated from direct participation in world affairs. Ultimately there will be more to gain in an 'open' economy inside a major bloc trading with other blocs. The so-called safety valve of London's grant has, in effect, become a limiting mechanism putting the brakes on creativity, potential and trading possibilities. This renders the North—with some very laudable exceptions— much too conservative, inexperienced and unprepared in *real* terms for the requirements and responsibilities of world trade. In addition, the North is carrying the extra burden of an inefficient and over-sized public service sector at a time when pressure is growing against bloated public services.

There are other aspects to the continued existence of the North in its current form which I believe are very restrictive. The following may not always affect the amount of money in the purse or pocket, but I believe they are very important:

The partition of Ireland cut northern Protestants off from so much of their own important history and identity, and no amount of artificial references to the 'Finchley factor' will ever compensate for that. Contrived attempts at creating a self-contained 'history of Northern Ireland' as if it were actually separate from people, events and society just a matter of miles down the road, has only compounded the problem. Ninety years of tragedy shaped by partition, while a sizeable minority looks beyond the six counties of Northern Ireland for a myriad of reasons, means that internal and external fractures will continue to strongly militate against ever constructing any sense of a nation, a country or even a region and community in 'the North' as we know it today.

At one level, saying 'you cannot partition the Battle of the Boyne from the Siege of Derry' might appear jingoistic; at another level, the very same statement becomes a precise and specific metaphor for how conjoined our stories in Ireland really are. But Protestants in the North have been separated from the rest of Ulster, never mind the rest of Ireland. In some senses they have separated themselves from their 'brothers and sisters' in, for example, the same Protestant churches. In trying to construct a solely N Ireland entity that is the immediate focus of their allegiance, they have separated themselves from a sense of place and story that truly reflects 400-plus years of being in Ireland. A restrictive and narrow 'Titanic only' vision of Northern Ireland is no replacement for the sense of place and history all Protestants have brought to *all* of Ireland.

Perhaps we need to be reminded that 'the Plantation of Ulster' in the 1600s wasn't restricted to just six counties; that the penal laws that affected Presbyterians affected them wherever they were in Ireland; that the potato famine did not miraculously miss what became 'the North'; that the names of the towns, villages and parishes the settlers came to live in were Irish in nature; that the St Patrick's Day tradition of sporting finals applies to all four provinces, and so on. To try and claim that the North is therefore a different place with a different history is simply a contrivance that doesn't add up. When one adds the belated 'Finchley factor' of the Thatcher era, it is no surprise that there has been a kaleidoscope of identity fractures and issues, not to mention of course the longstanding and debilitating 'siege mentality' of Ulster Unionism. Promoting an assumed 'British identity' as a method of denying Irishness rings hollow when held up against Unionists' cultural distance and mistrust of the British; promoting the 'Ulster-Scots' identity likewise runs up against considerable feelings of scorn that many northern Protestants have of that particular label; promoting the 'Ulster identity' is always going to be problematic inasmuch as a geographical third of the province of Ulster is outside the North; and promoting the 'Northern Irish' identity means sharing it, to a limited degree, with literally thousands of people who look well beyond the North for their Irish cultural identity and sense of nation.

I believe that the northern Protestant concept of being in 'a place apart' which has contributed so heavily to the aforementioned 'siege mentality' could be radically transformed in a united Ireland. Quite clearly there will be numerous practicalities to address, including approaching the whole project in a constructive manner that builds on general calls for a united Ireland. In the new Republic that I and many others envisage, everyone including northern Protestants would have the protections they deserve: individual dignity, the right to religious views, education, freedom of speech, no state religion and numerous social protections.

I know that we must travel some distance to increase our knowledge of each other: Protestant to Catholic in the North, Northerners of all hues

143

to Southerners of all hues, and all the new communities shaped in the union thereof. The vast majority of the two main communities in the North were shaped by separation at partition, then subsequent misrule and the tragedy of 'the Troubles'. In short it has been a negative and debilitating experience with very destructive results, and although, relatively speaking, things have improved greatly since those dark days, clearly, there is still much to be done. I therefore disagree profoundly that we have reached the level and point where we should simply 'leave things as they are' in 2012. I believe we can travel another distance whereby we can live in a truly united Ireland in which all people repair and build relationships that productively and completely restore all our rights and place on the island.

The 'second' or 'real' Irish republic could then take its place as a complete nation embracing all of Ireland, with all its diverse peoples, and be fit for twenty-first century purpose. I may be writing this in very difficult times in which negative headlines unfortunately shape a lot of public opinion but like President Michael D Higgins and the late Dr Garrett Fitzgerald, I have great faith that the Irish people will come through the present difficulties.

The next hundred years could therefore be much more progressive, with Ireland taking her rightful place as an outward-looking small nation, engaging dynamically and productively with other nations of the world. Instead of dragging the same old attitudes and jaded clichés into the future—along with all the negatives they represent—history could record the positive relations throughout Ireland, and the success stories of a forward-thinking people who finally embraced their shared destiny in a truly united Ireland.

Lightning Source UK Ltd.
Milton Keynes UK
UKOW050605100912

198741UK00001B/38/P